Rosa
Luxemburg

by Tony Cliff

BOOKMARKS

Third printing October 1986.
Bookmarks, 265 Seven Sisters Road, London N4 2DE, England.
Bookmarks, PO Box 16085, Chicago, Illinois 60616, USA.
Bookmarks, GPO Box 1473N, Melbourne 3001, Australia
First published May 1959.
Published by Bookmarks 1980. Reprinted 1983.

ISBN 0 906224 10 1

Printed by A Wheaton and Company, Exeter, England.
Cover design by Peter Court

 Bookmarks is the publisher for an international grouping of
socialist organisations:

AUSTRALIA: **International Socialists**, GPO Box 1473N,
Melbourne 3001.
BRITAIN: **Socialist Workers Party**, PO Box 82, London E3.
BELGIUM: **Socialisme International**, 9 rue Marexhe, 4400
Herstal, Liege.
CANADA: **International Socialists**, PO Box 339, Station E,
Toronto, Ontario.
DENMARK: **Internationale Socialister**, Morten Borupsgade 18,
kld, 8000 Arhus C.
FRANCE: **Socialisme International** (correspondence to Ives
Coleman, BP 407, Paris Cedex 05).
IRELAND: **Socialist Workers Movement**, PO Box 1648, Dublin 8.
NORWAY: **Internasjonale Sosialister**, Postboks 5370 Majorstua,
0304 Oslo 3.
UNITED STATES: **International Socialist Organization**, PO Box
16085, Chicago, Illinois 60616.
WEST GERMANY: **Sozialistische Arbeiter Gruppe**,
Wolfgangstrasse 81, 6000 Frankfurt 1.

Contents

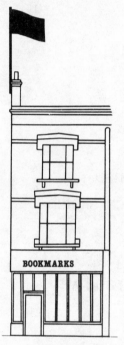

This is the eighth book to be published through the Bookmarks Publishing Co-operative, a group of socialists who have loaned money and contributed their skills.

Many socialists have a few savings put aside, probably in a bank or savings bank. While it's there, it's being loaned by the bank to some business or other to further the aims of capitalism. We believe that it is better to loan to a socialist venture to further the aims of socialism.

That's how the Bookmarks Publishing Co-operative works. In return for a loan, repayable at a month's notice, members receive free copies of books published, and other advantages. The co-op has over 120 members, from as near as London N5 and as far away as Australia and Canada.

Like to know more? Write to Bookmarks Publishing Co-operative, 265 Seven Sisters Road, London N4 2DE, England.

Author's foreword

On 15 January 1919, a soldier's rifle butt smashed the skull of Rosa Luxemburg, revolutionary genius, fighter and thinker. A personification of the unity of theory and practice, Rosa Luxemburg's life and work require a description of her activities as well as her thoughts — they are inseparable. In the framework of a small book, however, one cannot hope to do justice to both. In trying to avoid falling between two stools, this book concentrates mainly on Rosa Luxemburg's ideas, as they contain her main permanent contribution to the international socialist movement.

Little of her writing has been translated into English. It is, therefore, useful to give as varied a selection from her work (largely translated from the original German) as possible.

A scientific socialist, whose motto was 'doubt all', Rosa Luxemburg could have wished for nothing better than a critical evaluation of her own work. This book is written in a spirit of admiration and criticism of its subject.

Tony Cliff is a leading member of the Socialist Workers Party and the author of many publications, including **Lenin** (four volumes, 1979), **State Capitalism in Russia** (1955), and **Neither Washington nor Moscow** (selected essays, 1982).

Sources

Main sources quoted, with abbreviations where used:

Books by Rosa Luxemburg:

Acc **The Accumulation of Capital** (London 1951)

AR **Ausgewählte Reden und Schriften** (selected speeches and writings, two volumes, Berlin 1955)

GW **Gesammelte Werke** (Collected works, volumes 3, 4 and 6, Berlin)

RR **Reform or Revolution** (Bombay 1951)

Russ **The Russian Revolution** (New York 1940)

Books on Rosa Luxemburg:

Fr Paul Frölich, **Rosa Luxemburg**, her life and work (London 1940)

F Oelssner, **Rosa Luxemburg: Eine Kritische Biographische Skizze** (Rosa Luxemburg: A critical biographical sketch, Berlin 1956)

Other sources:

Documente **Dokumente und Materialen zur Geschichte der Deutschen Arbeiterbewegung** (Documents and material on the history of the German Labour Movement 1914–18, two volumes, Berlin 1957)

V I Lenin, **Selected Works** (London 1944)

V I Lenin, **Works** (in Russian, fourth edition)

NZ **Die Neue Zeit**, theoretical publication of the German Social Democratic Party

■ For publications on Rosa Luxemburg which are available today, see the suggested reading at the back of this book.

Introduction
by Lindsey German

When Rosa Luxemburg was murdered in 1919, her old adversary Karl Kautsky wrote: 'Rosa Luxemburg and her friends will always occupy an outstanding position in the history of socialism: but they represent an era that has come to an end'. He was completely wrong. The revolutionary tradition upheld by Rosa Luxemburg in Germany was to play a decisive role in the years immediately following her death.

For revolutionaries today, it is amazing how many of her ideas, and the political positions she fought for, remain relevant. So much of her analysis has been borne out by events, while the compromises and hesitations of those who opposed her during her lifetime (and their followers today) have also been shown at best to lead up blind alleys, at worst to disaster. Rosa Luxemburg delivered her first attack on the reformists in the 1890s, bitterly opposing the idea that capitalism could be neutralised and transformed to the benefit of workers. Today we still face reformist parties, some of them in government as in France or Spain. Rosa Luxemburg's arguments against them are still relevant.

Rosa Luxemburg said that the choice facing humanity was between 'socialism or barbarism'. She could not have imagined the barbarism of nuclear war, but her ideas help us in the fight against it. Capitalist competition in the age of imperialism, she argued, takes on more and more the form of military as well as economic competition, which is why the fight against militarism is not the separate or moral fight which the reformists then and today believed it to be, but a fight against the whole capitalist system.

Above all perhaps her greatest contribution was her understanding that the mass general strike was playing and would continue to play a more and more central role in the revolutionary transformation of society. Experience of revolutionary movements today, from Hungary in 1956 to France in 1968 and Chile in the early 70s, shows how correct that analysis was — yet it was either opposed or ignored during her lifetime.

All these ideas deal with some of the major problems facing socialists today. This is the reason for again reprinting Tony Cliff's small book on Rosa Luxemburg. When first written it was an attempt to make her basic ideas accessible to a new audience, unfamiliar with both the writings and the period in which Rosa Luxemburg wrote and acted. In that, it succeeds very well. We are given a clear introduction to her ideas, whether on the national question, reform and revolution, or the accumulation of capital. But simply to leave the book as it stands would give an incomplete assessment of Rosa Luxemburg's strengths and weaknesses.

The reason is straightforward enough. When the book was first written 25 years ago, its aim was to present Rosa Luxemburg's ideas in order to reassert the revolutionary socialist tradition. This tradition — that, in Marx's words, 'the emancipation of the working class is the act of the working class' — had all but disappeared after the 1920s. The gross bureaucratic structures of Stalinism in the east and the Communist or Socialist parties in the west produced a view that socialism was achieved by the few on behalf of the many. And in a strange way the small Trotskyist groups which did still uphold revolutionary ideas mirrored this approach. They took the view that the working class would eventually come to the 'correct' programme (theirs) and so make the revolution. In other words these groups felt they had nothing to learn from the working class or the day-to-day class struggle.

Rosa Luxemburg's ideas are particulaly refreshing against such a background. Time and again, she stresses that the socialist revolution is made by the spontaneous actions of the working class. Revolutionaries must learn from and try to generalise those actions.

Such ideas were completely foreign to the Stalinism which dominated at the time Cliff's book was written. The Stalinist parties believed that the party was there to represent and act on behalf of the working class. The class struggle was not seen as the activity of the working class itself, in which revolutionaries intervene to try to lead it in a revolutionary direction. Rather, action was to be decided on by the leadership of the party — and they would then try to get workers to agree to it. Spontaneous struggles, far from being welcomed, merely upset and often challenged the existing order of things.

Rosa Luxemburg herself faced exactly this attitude in the huge, passive and propagandist German socialist party, SPD, to which she belonged for most of her politically active life. But her polemics against this sort of organisation — formal, stultifying and ultimately willing to accept the capitalist system — have laid her open to many criticisms. Stalin and his followers characterised her ideas as 'spontaneist'. She just tailed along after workers' spontaneous struggles, they said, and didn't understand the role of socialist organisation in directing this struggle.

Such attacks are gross distortions of Rosa Luxemburg's views. She always stressed the importance of organisation (which is one of the major reasons she was so reluctant to break from the SPD). Not only that, from her teenage years she was always herself a member of socialist organisations, both in Poland and Germany. Even so, there is little doubt that her view of socialist organisation was often flawed and sometimes wrong. These failings had serious consequences for the direction of the German and Russian revolutions. It is therefore worth loking at Rosa Luxemburg's writings on class struggle, on revolutionary socialist organisation and on the relationship between the two in more detail. Cliff's original does not go into sufficient detail in this respect. Also, because it was written before the growth of the revolutionary left in Europe in the 1960s, and their subsequent ups and downs, it doesn't test recent experience against that of Rosa Luxemburg.

By far the best of Luxemburg's writings on class struggle is her pamphlet on the 1905 revolution in Russia, *The Mass Strike*. Here she tries to explain a new phenomenon — the general strike. Today the idea of a general strike is in no way strange — but in 1906 it was a bombshell. Hard to believe though it may seem now, the attitudes of socialists toward such strikes had always been extremely negative. It had always been the anarchists who had stressed the strike as the way to destroy capitalism — although they thought this was all that was required. Even when socialists accepted the strike as a tactic, they saw it as essentially defensive.

This was the position held by the SPD at the outbreak of revolution in Russia in 1905. Rosa Luxemburg's analysis of events and her conclusions presented a strong challenge to these ideas. They also provoked personal and political attacks from various SPD members, espcially the trade union leaders. She was already unpopular with them for her description of trade union activity as a 'labour of Sisyphus' (one that never ends). Now they were horrified that she was encouraging struggle which went far beyond the orderly approach of the German unions.

The Mass Strike was a new and unique recognition of the role of the strike in the revolutionary process. Rosa Luxemburg saw that as capitalism developed, the mass strike would become more and more central. Socialist revolution was not simply the takeover of the capitalist system by one group rather than another. It wasn't simply a change in the outward *political* forms. It was also — and had to be — an *economic* challenge by the workers which struck at the very heart of the capitalist system. *This* gave the workers their political power.

Rosa Luxemburg ridiculed the idea that there was a division between the political and economic struggle (an idea beloved of reformists then and now). Strikes can begin over seemingly trivial economic demands but rapidly generalise to become a challenge on a broader political level — against the government, the employers or the law. The other side of the coin, she said, is that political revolution has to become an economic challenge, otherwise it will ultimately fail — an argument to which she returned in the course of the German revolution of 1918–1919.

Rosa Luxemburg also attacked the idea that the strike should be called up or its course determined in a mechanical way. The party could not say when or how such a strike would materialise. 'The mass strike cannot be called at will, even when the decision to do so may come from the highest committee of the strongest Social Democratic party', she wrote. Nor could a revolutionary general strike arise in a period when there was no revolutionary potential.

The pamphlet was a celebration of the strikes and revolution in 'backward' Russia, a guide to action for revolutionaries and, by implication, an attack on the German party trade union leaders. Like the trade union bureaucracy today, they saw the general strike as a last resort, a pressurising tactic, rather than a necessary part of the revolutionary struggle.

Rosa Luxemburg emphasised throughout that the working class has to emancipate itself and there can be no blueprints laid down for the nature of this self-emancipation. In doing so she attacked bureaucratisation inside socialist parties. But in the process — although she always stressed the need for organisation — she never formulated what *sort* of organisation was needed. This proved a major weakness.

Like every other leading member of the Socialist Second International, Rosa Luxemburg was a product of her time and circumstances. The Social Democratic parties had grown in the last years of the 19th century, often into sizeable organisations. They adhered to the formal politics of Marx but often included in their ranks both reformists and revolutionaries — and those who swung between the two. The dominant belief was that socialism would arrive gradually and inevitably and therefore their main job was not intervention in the day-to-day class struggle but propaganda. The socialist strength of these parties was not often tested in practice — which meant they could contain all sorts of people who agreed about very little.

Rosa Luxemburg always understood, perhaps more sharply than any other, the dubious politics of many of those inside the German party. She also saw the need to take part in the day-to-day struggles of workers. But she never drew the organisational conclusions from this understanding. She believed until very late in her life that there was no alternative to remaining inside the SPD.

It was left to the Russsian Bolsheviks and Lenin — part of a much smaller socialist movement — to develop a form of organisation which was able to intervene much more successfully and eventually to lead the Russian working class to take state power. In 1903, the Russian Social Democratic party split over a seemingly trivial issue — whether party members should work under the discipline of the party, or whether conditions of membership should be much looser. The two parties resulting from the split were known as the Bolsheviks and the Mensheviks.

Rosa Luxemburg attacked the split and Lenin's concept of a disciplined 'democratic centralist' party. She recognised, with Lenin, the special circumstances in Russia — a backward economy, tiny working class and autocratic, repressive government — but argued that none of these should lead to centralised party organisation. She said such 'ultra-centralism' would cut the Russian party off from the working class.

Lenin, on the other hand, argued that precisely because of these conditions the working class would not be able to achieve socialist revolution without such a party. A loose, flabby party of the sort which existed in Germany would not do (although Lenin himself did not believe until much later that the form of organisation in Germany itself was wrong). He therefore set out to build a disciplined organisation which implemented decisions, once they were democratically decided, in a unified and coherent manner.

Rosa Luxemburg was not the only person to attack him. Many well-known socialists, in Russia and abroad, did so too. He was accused of being unnecessarily sectarian, of narrowing the base of the party, and of wanting to set up a minority 'Jacobin' dictatorship. In explanation he wrote in 1903: 'We argued that the concept "Party member" must be *narrowed* so as to separate those who worked from those who merely talked, to eliminate organisational chaos, to eliminate the monstrous and absurd possibility of there being organisations which consisted of Party members but which were not Party organisations'.

A revolutionary party had to have unity in action, he said, and this demanded as a precondition theoretical clarity and political understanding. 'Achieving ideological unity = propagating definite ideas, *clarifying* class differences, effecting ideological demarcation . . . propagating ideas *that can lead forward*, the ideas of the progressive class.'

What Lenin managed to achieve in building such a party was precisely to test party members *in practice*. This meant that during the 'dress rehearsal' revolution of 1905 the Bolsheviks were not only able to intervene, but they were also able to learn the lessons of the mass strikes, of the new *soviets* or workers' councils which had sprung up from this struggle, and of the role of the party in these organisations. And although that party declined in the years of reaction which followed, it was able to hold together as a coherent force, even when it had little support. And its success was to show in 1917.

The revolution of February 1917 broke out in Russia in the way described earlier by Rosa Luxemburg in *The Mass Strike* — through the mass spontaneous upsurge of workers' struggles. It was not led by the Bolsheviks — indeed they were taken by surprise. But the test of the party was how it could relate to, generalise and spread these struggles. Here, because of its structures, organisations and political clarity, it was able to assess the class nature of the revolution, to hold back the most advanced sections of the class from moving towards a premature rising in July, to help repel the attempted right-wing coup by Kornilov in August, and to lead the successful October insurrection.

In other words, at every crucial point in the revolutionary process — when the success of workers' power hung in the balance — the Bolshevik party was able to act decisively to lead it to success.

Soviet power in Russia led to a revolutionary wave throughout Europe. This was essential. Lenin himself believed that 'without a revolution in Germany we shall perish'. Russia was too economically backward to sustain socialism alone. All eyes looked to Germany, the major capitalist power with the strongest workers' movement and the largest socialist party. But that party had already shown that far from being committed to socialist revolution, it was prepared to go to great lengths to prop up the capitalist system.

Rosa Luxemburg had become increasingly aware of this. She had argued vehemently with various groups inside the party — with the 'revisionists', the trade union leaders, the 'gradualists'. But the nature of the SPD was such that these arguments remained purely at the level of argument. They therefore usually remained above the heads of the ordinary workers and party members that she needed to influence. So she remained in a minority.

Such political arguments also became increasingly divorced from the party rank and file. Far from the party being the vehicle which aimed to combat ruling class ideas, it became a party which *reflected* these ideas. This was against everything Rosa Luxemburg stood for. But she recoiled from the idea of setting up any alternative party. She remained inside the SPD, despite increasing isolation in the years before the outbreak of war in 1914. She did form a small group of co-thinkers to combat the rightward drift of the party, but it remained a propaganda group and didn't build real links with party workers.

The betrayal of the SPD leadership in supporting the war of German imperialism in 1914 probably didn't come as a total surprise to Rosa Luxemburg. After all, their reaction to the Morocco crisis in 1911 had been similar, if less serious. What came as a much greater shock was the almost universal support for the leadership among the party members and in the working-class movement. Suport for Rosa Luxemburg's stand against the war could be counted among a few individuals only — the result of her political isolation.

Even then, however, Rosa Luxemburg didn't break from the party. Only in 1917, when the Independents broke away under the pressure of anti-war feeling and formed their own organisation, did she also leave. And only on her release from prison in the last months of 1918 did she set out to build a party on the Bolshevik model — the German Communist Party (KPD). Even this she did reluctantly, feeling that the embryo party was too immature to develop.

Why did Rosa Luxemburg not follow the Bolshevik pattern and build an independent revolutionary party?

Firstly, no one thought that the theories developed by Lenin applied generally before 1917. This special form of organisation, they said, applied only to the specific conditions in Russia. Secondly, the German SPD to which Rosa Luxemburg belonged was by far the largest and most impressive workers' party in the world. The idea of splitting from it would have filled most people with horror. And because in practice the dominant view of politics was propaganda, it obviously made more sense to put out your ideas from a large party than from a small one.

But it was also the case that Rosa Luxemburg relied very heavily on the power of intellectual argument. This meant she believed that although revolutionary ideas might be in a minority at certain periods, the working class would look to those ideas when the revolution arrived. In a sense this was obviously true. And in 1918–19 millions of German workers did look for revolutionary ideas. But they didn't look to Rosa Luxemburg and the new KPD, they looked to the old party and its leaders — people who were prepared to talk left-wing ideas at such a time, but whose past words and deeds told a very different story. Rosa Luxemburg had been consistently principled in her revolutionary politics — but this fact wasn't known to the mass of workers for she had remained largely hidden in the SPD.

Belief in the power of intellectual argument can also lead to a certain abstention from the day-to-day running and building of a party. The other party to which Rosa belonged — and which she had helped to form much more than the SPD — the Polish Socialist Party, gave some inkling of this. Her biographer John Nettl notes that the Polish party's leaflets during the 1905 revolution were far more intellectual and abstract than those of the Bolsheviks, and far less in touch with workers' struggle.

This wasn't completely accidental. It stemmed from an idea of the party as something which developed fully fledged rather than growing out of the experience of its members in the everyday struggle. The Polish leader Leo Jogiches, Rosa Luxemburg's lover and life-long collaborator, expressed doubts at the formation of the KPD in 1918 because of its lack of maturity (an undeniable fact). It was as though he expected political maturity to appear magically to fit the situation, rather than seeing it as developing only as the party withstands the tests of time and intervention.

This failure to build a revolutionary socialist party early enough had a terrible impact on the German revolution. Unlike Lenin, Rosa Luxemburg had no organisation which could be tried and tested in the course of small disputes before being thrown into the heat of revolution. So the newly formed KPD could not take full advantage of the revolutionary opportunities of 1918–19.

And Rosa Luxemburg herself suffered from her failure to build such a party. No socialist can remain indefinitely an isolated if talented individual without suffering political distortions. This was precisely the role she adopted for much of her political life. She showed great courage in speaking out and acting against the party leadership — but as an individual. Lenin wrote of *The Junius Pamphlet* (before he knew Rosa Luxemburg was its author): 'Junius's pamphlet conjures up in our mind the picture of a *lone* man who has no comrades in an illegal organisation accustomed to thinking out revolutionary slogans to their conclusion and systematically educating the masses in their spirit.'

Rosa Luxemburg's understanding of the problems facing the German revolution was acute when she emerged from prison in November 1918. She also understood the need to build a revolutionary socialist party. But because she acted as an individual she had a tendency to blur her political clarity in public, in order, she felt, not to alienate the best sections of the working class.

Lenin and the Bolsheviks, with experienced members in the factories, members who were tried, tested and respected because of years of hard class struggle, could criticise the action of workers during the ferment of revolution — for example holding workers back from what would have been a disastrous premature rising in July 1917 — because these members could carry and win the argument within the working class. But Rosa Luxemburg's isolation, her failure to build a revolutionary socialist party years earlier, meant that she lacked this solid base on which to stand. She was reluctant to criticise for fear of being seen as abandoning workers in the heat of struggle. Yet such criticism was vitally needed, as the premature rising of German workers in January 1919 was to show.

The result was a terrible personal and political tragedy. Rosa Luxemburg, Karl Liebknecht and many others paid with their lives. But the tragedy was not just theirs. In a short space of years, the lack of a party in Germany led to the defeat of the German Revolution, followed by the defeat of socialist hopes on a world scale, the growth of fascism in Germany and of Stalinism in Russia. Rosa Luxemburg's stirring defence of workers' spontaneous struggles was not enough when those struggles erupted and needed to be harnessed to the challenging and taking of state power.

Rosa Luxemburg has had the misfortune since her death to be praised by all sorts of people who would run a mile at the mention of revolution. Her stress on spontaneity and what the Stalinists claim was her downgrading of organisation has led to compliments from those as far away from her politics as Labour Party leaders Eric Heffer and Michael Foot. She would have been disgusted by such praise, because had they been members of the German SPD she would have denounced them time and again. She would also be shocked by those who today try to use some of her writings to justify attacks on Lenin's ideas on the party. Those who doubt this should read her attacks — for example the article *Either/Or* — on those who believe there is some middle road between reform and revolution.

Rosa Luxemburg stood clearly in the tradition of revolutionary socialism, of internationalism and of workers' self-emancipation.

Rosa Luxemburg:Biographical Sketch

Rosa Luxemburg was born in the small Polish town of Zamosc on 5 March, 1871. From early youth she was active in the socialist movement. She joined a revolutionary party called *Proletariat*, founded in 1882, some 21 years before the Russian Social-Democratic Party (Bolsheviks and Mensheviks) came into being. From the beginning *Proletariat* was, in principles and programme, many steps ahead of the revolutionary movement in Russia. While the Russian revolutionary movement was still restricted to acts of individual terrorism carried out by a few heroic intellectuals, *Proletariat* was organising and leading thousands of workers on strike. In 1886, however, *Proletariat* was practically decapitated by the execution of four of its leaders, the imprisonment of 23 others for long terms of hard labour, and the banishment of about two hundred more. Only small circles were saved from the wreck, and it was one of these that Rosa Luxemburg joined at the age of 16. By 1889 the police had caught up with her, and she had to leave Poland, her comrades thinking she could do more useful work abroad than in prison. She went to Switzerland, to Zurich, which was the most important centre of Polish and Russian emigration. There she entered the university where she studied natural sciences, mathematics and economics. She took an active part in the local labour movement and in the intense intellectual life of the revolutionary emigrants.

Hardly more than a couple of years later, Rosa Luxemburg was already recognised as the theoretical leader of the revolutionary socialist party of Poland. She became the main contributor to the party paper, *Sprawa Rabotnicza*, published in Paris. In 1894 the name of the party, *Proletariat*, was changed to become the Social-Democratic Party of the

Kingdom of Poland; shortly afterwards Lithuania was added to the title. Rosa continued to be the theoretical leader of the Party (the SDKPL) till the end of her life.

In August, 1893, she represented the party at the Congress of the Socialist International. There, a young woman of 22, she had to contend with well-known veterans of another Polish party, the Polish Socialist Party (PPS), whose main plank was the independence of Poland and which claimed the recognition of all the experienced elders of inter-national socialism. Support for the national movement in Poland had the weight of long tradition behind it; Marx and Engels, too, had made it an important plank in their policies. Undaunted by all this, Rosa Luxemburg struck out at the PPS, accusing it of clear nationalistic tendencies and a proneness to diverting the workers from the path of class struggle; and she dared to take a different position to the old masters and oppose the slogan of independence for Poland. (For an elaboration of Rosa Luxemburg's position on the national question, see Chapter 6). Her adversaries heaped abuse on her, some of them, like the veteran disciple and friend of Marx and Engels, Wilhelm Liebknecht, going so far as to accuse her of being an agent of the Tsarist secret police. But she stuck to her point.

Intellectually she grew by leaps and bounds. She was drawn irresistibly to the centre of the international labour movement, Germany, where she made her way in 1898.

She started writing assiduously, and after a time became one of the main contributors to the most important Marxist theoretical journal of the time, *Die Neue Zeit*. Invariably independent in judgment and criticism, even the tremendous prestige of Karl Kautsky, its editor, 'the Pope of Marxism' as he used to be called, did not deflect her from her considered opinions, once she had become convinced.

Rosa Luxemburg entered heart and soul into the labour movement in Germany. She was a regular contributor to a number of socialist papers—in some cases their editor—she addressed many mass meetings and took part energetically in all the tasks the movement called upon her to perform. Throughout, her speeches and articles were original creative works, in which she appealed to reason rather than emotion, and in which she always opened up to her readers a wider and grander horizon than they had known before.

At that time the movement in Germany was split into two main trends, one reformist and the other revolutionary, with the former grow-ing in strength. Germany had enjoyed continuous prosperity since the slump of 1873. The workers' standard of living had improved uninter-ruptedly, if slowly; trade unions and co-operatives grew stronger.

Against this background, the bureaucracy of these movements, together with the increasing parliamentary representation of the Social Democratic Party, moved away from revolution and lent great strength to those who were already proclaiming gradualism, or reformism as their principle. The main spokesman of this trend was Eduard Bernstein, a disciple of Engels. Between 1896 and 1898 he wrote a series of articles in *Die Neue Zeit* on 'Problems of Socialism,' more and more openly attacking the principles of Marxism. A long and bitter discussion broke out. Rosa Luxemburg, who had just entered the German labour movement, immediately sprang to the defence of Marxism. Brilliantly and with magnificent drive, she attacked the spreading cancer of reformism in her booklet, *Social Reform or Social Revolution*. (For an elaboration of her criticism of Reformism, see Chapter 2).

Soon afterwards, in 1899, the French 'Socialist' Millerand, entered a coalition government with a capitalist party. Rosa Luxemburg followed this experiment closely and analysed it in a series of brilliant articles dealing with the situation in the French labour movement in general, and the question of coalition governments in particular (see Chapter 2). After the fiasco of Macdonald in Britain, of the Weimar Republic in Germany, of the Popular Front in France in the 'thirties and the post-Second World War coalition governments in the same country, it is clear that the lessons drawn by Rosa Luxemburg are not of historical interest alone.

In 1903-4 Rosa Luxemburg indulged in a polemic with Lenin, with whom she disagreed on the national question (see Chapter 6), and on the conception of party structure and the relation between the party and the activity of the masses (see Chapter 5).

In 1904, after 'insulting the Kaiser' she was sentenced to three months' imprisonment, of which she served a month.

In 1905, with the outbreak of the first Russian Revolution, she wrote a series of articles and pamphlets for the Polish Party, in which she developed the idea of the permanent revolution, which had been independently developed by Trotsky and Parvus but was held by few Marxists of the time. While both the Mensheviks and Bolsheviks, despite the deep cleavage between them, believed that the Russian Revolution was to be a bourgeois democratic one, Rosa argued that it would develop beyond the stage of bourgeois democracy and would either end in workers' power or complete defeat. Her slogan was 'revolutionary dictatorship of the proletariat based on the peasantry.'[*]

---

[*] It was not for nothing that Stalin denounced Luxemburg posthumously in 1931 as a Trotskyist. (See J V Stalin *Works* Vol XIII, pp. 86-104).

However, to think, write and speak about the revolution was not enough for Rosa Luxemburg. The motto of her life was: 'At the beginning was the deed.' And although she was in bad health at the time, she smuggled herself into Russian Poland as soon as she was able to do so (in December 1905). The zenith of the revolution had by then passed. The masses were still active, but were now hesitant while reaction was raising its head. All meetings were forbidden, but the workers still held meetings in their strongholds, the factories. All workers' papers were suppressed, but Rosa Luxemburg's party paper continued to appear daily, although printed clandestinely. On 4 March, 1906, she was arrested and kept for four months, first in prison, then in a fortress. Thereafter she was freed, on the grounds of ill health and her German nationality, and expelled from the country.

The Russian revolution of 1905 gave flesh and blood to an idea Rosa Luxemburg had conceived some years earlier: that mass strikes—political and economic—constitute a cardinal element in the revolutionary workers' struggle for power, distinguishing socialist from all previous revolutions. Now she elaborated the idea on the basis of a new historical experience. (See Chapter 3).

Speaking to this effect at a public meeting, she was accused of 'inciting to violence' and spent another two months in prison, this time in Germany.

In 1907 she participated in the Congress of the Socialist International held in Stuttgart. She spoke in the name of the Russian and Polish parties, developing a consistent revolutionary attitude to imperialist war and militarism. (See Chapter 4).

Between 1905 and 1910 the split widened between Rosa Luxemburg and the centrist leadership of the SPD, of which Kautsky was the theoretical mouthpiece. Already in 1907 Rosa Luxemburg had expressed her fear that the party leaders, notwithstanding their profession of Marxism, would flinch before a situation in which decisive action was called for. The climax came in 1910, with a complete break between Rosa Luxemburg and Karl Kautsky on the question of the workers' road to power. From now on the SPD was split into three separate tendencies: the reformists, who progressively adopted an imperialist policy; the so-called Marxist centre, led by Kautsky (now nick-named by Luxemburg the 'leader of the swamp') which kept its verbal radicalism but confined itself more and more to parliamentary methods of struggle; and the revolutionary wing, of which Rosa Luxemburg was the main inspiration.

In 1913 Rosa Luxemburg published her most important theoretical work, *The Accumulation of Capital. A Contribution to the Economic*

Explanation of Imperialism. This is, without doubt, one of the most original contributions to Marxist economic doctrine since *Capital.* In its wealth of knowledge, brilliance of style, trenchancy of analysis and intellectual independence, this book, as Mehring, Marx's biographer, stated, was the nearest to *Capital* of any Marxist work. The central problem it studies is of tremendous theoretical and political import-ance: namely, what effects the extension of capitalism into new, backward territories has on the internal contradictions rending capitalism and on the stability of the system. (For an analysis of this work, see Chapter 8).

On 20 February, 1914, Rosa Luxemburg was arrested for inciting soldiers to mutiny. The basis of the charge was a speech in which she declared: 'If they expect us to murder our French or other foreign brothers, then let us tell them: "No, under no circumstances".' In court she turned from defendant into prosecutor, and her speech, published later under the title *Militarism, War and the Working Class*, is one of the most inspiring revolutionary socialist condemnations of imperialism. She was sentenced to a year's imprisonment but was not detained on the spot. On leaving the courtroom she immediately went to a mass meeting at which she repeated her revolutionary anti-war propaganda.

When the First World War broke out, practically all the leaders of the Socialist Party were swept into the patriotic tide. On 3 August, 1914, the parliamentary group of German Social Democracy decided to vote in favour of war credits for the Kaiser's government. Of the 111 deputies only 15 showed any desire to vote against. However, after their request for permission to do so had been rejected, they submitted to party discipline, and on 4 August the whole Social Democratic group unanim-ously voted in favour of the credits. A few months later, on 2 December, Karl Liebknecht flouted party discipline to vote with his conscience. His was the sole vote against war credits.

This decision of the party leadership was a cruel blow to Rosa Luxemburg. However, she did not give way to despair. On the same day, 4 August, on which the Social Democratic deputies rallied to the Kaiser's banner, a small group of socialists met in her apartment and decided to take up the struggle against the war. This group, led by Luxemburg, Karl Liebknecht, Franz Mehring and Klara Zetkin, ultimately became the Spartakus League. For four years, mainly from prison, Rosa continued to lead, inspire and organise the revolutionaries, keeping high the banner of international socialism. (For further details of her anti-war policy, see Chapter 4).

The outbreak of the war cut Rosa Luxemburg off from the Polish labour movement, but she must have gained deep satisfaction from the fact that her own Polish party remained loyal throughout to the ideas of international socialism.

The Revolution in Russia of February 1917 was a realisation of Rosa Luxemburg's policy of revolutionary opposition to the war and struggle for the overthrow of imperialist governments. Feverishly she followed the events from prison, studying them closely in order to draw lessons for the future. Unhesitatingly she stated that the February victory was not the end of the struggle, but only its beginning, that only workers' power could assure peace. From prison she issued call after call to the German workers and soldiers to emulate their Russian brethren, overthrow the Junkers and capitalists and thus, while serving the Russian Revolution, at the same time prevent themselves from bleeding to death under the ruins of capitalist barbarism.

When the October Revolution broke out, Rosa Luxemburg welcomed it enthusiastically, praising it in the highest terms. At the same time she did not believe that uncritical acceptance of everything the Bolsheviks did would be of service to the labour movement. She clearly foresaw that if the Russian Revolution remained in isolation, a number of distortions would cripple its development; and quite early in the development of Soviet Russia she pointed out such distortions, particularly on the question of democracy. (See Chapter 7).

On 8 November, 1918, the German Revolution freed Rosa Luxemburg from prison. With all her energy and enthusiasm she threw herself into the revolution. Unfortunately the forces of reaction were strong. Right-wing Social-Democratic leaders and generals of the old Kaiser's army joined forces to suppress the revolutionary working class. Thousands of workers were murdered; on 15 January, 1919, Karl Liebknecht was killed; on the same day a soldier's rifle butt smashed into Rosa Luxemburg's skull.

With her death the international workers' movement lost one of its noblest souls. 'The finest brain amongst the scientific successors of Marx and Engels,' as Mehring said, was no more. In her life, as in her death, she gave everything for the liberation of humanity.

Reform or Revolution

Running through Rosa Luxemburg's entire work was the struggle against reformism, which narrowed down the aims of the labour movement to tinkering with capitalism instead of overthrowing it by revolutionary means. The most prominent spokesman of reformism (or revisionism, as it was known then) against whom Rosa first took up arms was Eduard Bernstein. She refuted his views with special incisiveness in her pamphlet, *Social Reform or Social Revolution*, which was made up of two series of articles published in the *Leipziger Volkszeitung*, the first in September, 1898, as an answer to Bernstein's articles in *Die Neue Zeit*, the second in April, 1899, in answer to his book, *The Preconditions of Socialism and the Tasks of Social Democracy*.

Bernstein redefined the fundamental character of the labour movement as a 'democratic socialist reform party' and not a party of social revolution. Opposing Marx, he argued that the contradictions in capitalism do not get sharper, but are continually being alleviated; capitalism is steadily being tamed, steadily becoming more adaptable. Cartels, trusts and credit institutions gradually regularise the anarchic nature of the system, so that instead of recurring slumps as visualised by Marx, there is a tendency towards permanent prosperity. Social contradictions are also weakened, according to Bernstein, by the viability of the middle class and the more democratic distribution of capital ownership through stock companies. The adaptability of the system to the needs of the time is shown also in the improvement of the economic, social and political condition of the working class as a result of the activities of the trade unions and co-operatives.

From this analysis Bernstein concluded that the socialist party must devote itself to bettering gradually the conditions of the working class and not to the revolutionary conquest of political power.

In opposition to Bernstein, Rosa Luxemburg argued that capitalist monopoly organisations (cartels and trusts) and credit institutions tend to deepen the antagonisms in capitalism and not to mitigate them. She describes their function: 'In a general way, cartels . . . appear . . . as a determined phase of capitalist development, which in the last analysis aggravates the anarchy of the capitalist world and expresses and ripens its internal contradictions. Cartels aggravate the antagonism existing between the mode of production and exchange by sharpening the struggle between the producer and consumer . . . They aggravate, furthermore, the antagonism existing between the mode of production and the mode of appropriation by opposing, in the most brutal fashion, to the working class the superior force of organised capital, and thus increasing the antagonism between Capital and Labour.

'Finally, capitalist combinations aggravate the contradiction existing between the international character of capitalist world economy and the national character of the State—insofar as they are always accompanied by a general tariff war, which sharpens the differences among the capitalist States. We must add to this the decidedly revolutionary influence exercised by cartels on the concentration of production, technical progress, etc.

'In other words, when evaluated from the angle of their final effect on capitalist economy, cartels and trusts fail as 'means of adaptation.' They fail to attenuate the contradictions of capitalism. On the contrary, they appear to be an instrument of greater anarchy. They encourage the further development of the internal contradictions of capitalism. They accelerate the coming of a general decline of capitalism.' (*RR,* pp. 14-15.)

Credit, too, said Rosa Luxemburg, far from circumventing the capitalist crisis, actually deepened it. The two most important functions of credit are to expand production and facilitate exchange, both of which functions aggravate the instability of the system. Capitalist economic crises develop as a result of the contradictions between production's permanent tendency to expand, and the limited consumption capacity of the capitalist market. Credit, by encouraging production on the one hand, encourages the tendency towards overproduction, and, being itself subject to grave instability in adverse circumstances, tends to shake the economy more and deepen the crisis. The role of credit in encouraging speculation is another factor increasing the instability of the capitalist mode of production.

Bernstein's trump card in support of his argument that the contradictions of capitalism were decreasing was that for two decades, since 1873, capitalism had not suffered a major slump. But, in Rosa Luxemburg's words, 'Hardly had Bernstein rejected, in 1898, Marx's theory of crises, when a profound general crisis broke out in 1900, while seven years later, a new crisis, beginning in the United States, hit the world market. Facts proved the theory of 'adaptation' to be false. They showed at the same time that the people who abandoned Marx's theory of crisis only because no crisis occurred within a certain space of time merely confused the essence of this theory with one of its secondary exterior aspects—the ten-year cycle. The description of the cycle of modern capitalist industry as a ten-year period was to Marx and Engels, in 1860 and 1870, only a simple statement of facts. It was not based on a natural law but on a series of given historic circumstances that were connected with the rapidly spreading activity of young capitalism.' (*RR*, p.15.) In fact, 'Crises may repeat themselves every five or ten years, or even every eight or twenty years . . . The belief that capitalist production could 'adapt' itself to exchange presupposes one of two things: either the world market can spread unlimitedly, or on the contrary the development of the productive forces is so fettered that it cannot pass beyond the bounds of the market. The first hypothesis constitutes a material impossibility. The second is rendered just as impossible by the constant technical progress that daily creates new productive forces in all branches.' (*RR*, p. 16)

As a matter of fact, Rosa Luxemburg argued, what is basic to Marxism is that the contradictions in capitalism—between the rising productive forces and the relations of production—are becoming progressively aggravated. But that these contradictions should express themselves in a catastrophic general crisis 'is of secondary importance' only . (*RR*, p. 7.) The form of expression of the fundamental contradiction is not as important as its content. (By the way, Rosa Luxemburg would in all probability not dispute the idea that one form in which the basic contradictions can express themselves is in the permanent war economy with its tremendous wastage of the productive forces.)

Rosa Luxemburg argued that when Bernstein denied the deepening contradictions within capitalism he cut away the basis of the struggle for socialism. Socialism thus became transformed from an economic necessity into a hoped-for ideal, a Utopia. Bernstein complained: 'Why represent socialism as the consequence of economic compulsion?' 'Why degrade man's understanding, his feeling for justice, his will?' (*Vorwaerts,* 26 March, 1899.) Rosa Luxemburg commented: Bernstein's superlatively just distribution is to be attained thanks to man's free will, man's will acting not because of economic necessity, since this will itself is only an instrument, but because of man's comprehension of justice, because of man's idea of justice.

'We thus quite happily return to the principle of justice, to the old war horse on which the reformers of the earth have rocked for ages, for the lack of surer means of historic transportation. We return to that lamentable Rosinante on which the Don Quixotes of history have galloped towards the great reform of the earth, always to come home with their eyes blackened.' (RR, p. 52.) Abstracted from the contradictions of capitalism, the urge towards socialism becomes merely an idealistic chimera.

Eduard Bernstein (and many after him) looked upon the trade unions as a weapon weakening capitalism. Rosa Luxemburg, in contradistinction, argued that while trade unions can somewhat affect the level of wages, they cannot by themselves overthrow the wages system, and the basic objective economic factors determining the wage level. 'Trade unions are nothing more than the organised defence of labour power against the attacks of profit. They express the resistance offered by the working class to the oppression of capitalist economy.

' . . . trade unions have the function of influencing the situation in the labour-power market. But this influence is being constantly overcome by the proletarianisation of the middle layers of our society, a process which continually brings new merchandise on the labour market. The second function of the trade unions is to ameliorate the condition of the workers. That is, they attempt to increase the share of the social wealth going to the working class. This share, however, is being reduced, with the fatality of a natural process, by the growth of the productivity of labour . . .

'In other words, the objective conditions of capitalist society transform the two economic functions of the trade unions into a sort of labour of Sisyphus,* which is, nevertheless, indispensable. For, as a result of the activity of his trade unions, the worker succeeds in obtaining for himself the rate of wages due to him in accordance with the situation of the labour-power market. As a result of trade union activity, the capitalist law of wages is applied and the effect of the depressing tendency of economic development is paralysed, or, to be more exact, is attenuated.' (RR, pp. 50-51.)

---

* The mythological king of Corinth who in the lower world was condemned to roll to the top of a hill a huge stone, which constantly rolled back again, making his task never-ending.

A labour of Sisyphus! This expression enraged the German trade union bureaucrats. They could not admit that the trade union struggle, however useful in protecting the workers from the imminent tendency of capitalism to depress their standards progressively, is not a substitute for the liberation of the working class.

While for Bernstein the trade unions (and co-operatives) were the main economic levers for achieving socialism, parliamentary democracy was the political lever for this transition. According to him parliament was the embodiment of society's will, in other words, it was an above-class institution.

Rosa Luxemburg, however, argues: '. . . the present State is not 'society' representing the 'rising working class.' It is itself the representative of capitalist society. It is a class State.' (*RR*, p. 22.) 'All in all, parliamentarism is not a directly socialist element impregnating gradually the whole capitalist society. It is, on the contrary, a specific form of the bourgeois class State.' (*RR*, pp. 29-30.)

At the time that the dispute about the parliamentary road to socialism was at its height in Germany, what they believed to be the conquest of political power through parliament was achieved for the first time by French socialists. In June, 1899, Alexandre Millerand entered the Radical government of Waldeck-Rousseau, sitting side by side with General Galliffet, butcher in chief of the Paris Commune. This action was acclaimed by the French socialist leader Jaurés and the right-wing reformists as a great tactical turning point: political power was now wielded no more by the bourgeoisie alone, but jointly by the bourgeoisie and the working class, which situation, according to them, was a political expression of the transition from capitalism to socialism.

Rosa followed this first experiment in coalition government between capitalist and socialist parties with close attention, making an extremely thorough investigation of it. She pointed out that this coalition, by binding the working class hand and foot to the government, prevented the workers from showing their real power. And in fact, what the opportunists called 'arid opposition' was a much more useful and practical policy: ' . . . far from rendering real, immediate, and tangible reforms a progressive character impossible, an oppositional policy is the only way in which minority parties in general and socialist minority parties in particular can obtain practical successes.' (*Fr*, p. 84.) The socialist party should take only those positions which give scope for anti-capitalist struggle: 'Of course, in order to be effective, Social Democracy must take all the positions she can in the present State and invade everywhere. However, the prerequisite for this is that these positions make it possible to wage the class struggle from them, the struggle against the bourgeoisie and its State.' (*AR,* II, p. 61.)

And she concluded: 'In the bourgeois society the role of Social Democracy is that of **opposition party.** As a **ruling party** it is allowed to rise only on the ruins of the bourgeois State.' (*AR,* p. 64.)

The final dangers inherent in the coalition experiment were pointed to: 'Jaurés, the tireless defender of the republic, is preparing the way for Caesarism. It sounds like a bad joke, but the course of history is strewn with such jokes.' (*Fr,* p. 84.)

How prophetic! The fiasco of Macdonald in Britain, the replacement of the Weimar republic by Hitler, the bankruptcy of the Popular Front in the 'thirties and the coalition governments in France after the Second World War, leading to de Gaulle, are some of the final fruits of the policy of coalition government.

To the reformists, who believed that parliamentarism and bourgeois legality meant the end of violence as a factor in historical development, Rosa countered: 'What is actually the whole function of bourgeois legality? If one 'free citizen' is taken by another against his will and confined in close and uncomfortable quarters for a while, everyone realises immediately that an act of violence has been committed. However, as soon as the process takes place in accordance with the book known as the penal code, and the quarters in question are in prison, then the whole affair immediately becomes peaceable and legal. If one man is compelled by another to kill his fellow men, then that is obviously an act of violence. However, as soon as the process is called 'military service,' the good citizen is consoled with the idea that everything is perfectly legal and in order. If one citizen is deprived against his will by another of some part of his property or earnings it is obvious that an act of violence has been committed, but immediately the process is called 'indirect taxation,' then everything is quite all right.

'In other words, what presents itself to us in the cloak of bourgeois legality is nothing but the expression of class violence raised to an obligatory norm by the ruling class. Once the individual act of violence has been raised in this way to an obligatory norm the process is reflected in the mind of the bourgeois lawyer (and no less in the mind of the socialist opportunist) not as it really is, but upside down: the legal process appears as an independent creation of abstract 'Justice,' and State compulsion appears as a consequence, as a mere 'sanctioning' of the law. In reality the truth is exactly the opposite: bourgeois legality (and parliamentarism as the legislature in process of development) is nothing but the particular social form in which the political violence of the bourgeoisie, developing its given economic basis, expresses itself.' (*GW,* III, pp. 361-2.)

Hence the idea of superceding capitalism by means of the legal forms established by capitalism itself, which, at bottom, are nothing but the expression of bourgeois violence, is absurd. In the final analysis, for the overthrow of capitalism, revolutionary violence is necessary: 'The use of violence will always remain the **ultima ratio** for the working class, the supreme law of the class struggle, always present, sometimes in a latent, sometimes in an active form. And when we try to revolutionise minds by parliamentary and other activity, it is only in order that at need the revolution may move not only the mind but also the hand.' (*GW*, III, p. 366.)

How prophetic now, after the demise of the Weimar Republic to be followed by the Nazis, were the following words of Rosa Luxemburg written in 1902: 'If Social Democracy were to accept the opportunist standpoint, renounce the use of violence, and pledge the working class never to diverge from the path of bourgeois legalism, then its whole parliamentary and other activity would sooner or later collapse miserably and leave the field to the untrammelled dominance of reactionary violence.' (*GW*, III, p. 366.)

But though Rosa Luxemburg knew that the workers were compelled to resort to revolutionary violence against exploitation and oppression, she suffered keenly the pain of every drop of blood shed. She wrote during the middle of the German revolution: 'Rivers of blood streamed during the four years of imperialist murder of nations [the First World War] . Now we must be sure to preserve every drop of this precious liquid with honour and in crystal glasses. Uncurbed revolutionary energy and wide human feeling—this is the real breath of socialism. It is true a whole world has to be overturned, but any tear that could have been avoided is an accusation; a man who hastens to perform an important deed and unthinkingly treads upon a worm on his way is committing a crime.' (*Rote Fahne,* 18 November, 1918.)

Among reformists as well as some who claim to be revolutionaries the theory is prevalent that only hunger may cause workers to follow a revolutionary path: the better-off workers of Central and Western Europe, argued the reformists, could therefore learn very little from the hungry and down-trodden Russian workers. Rosa Luxemburg made a big point of correcting this wrong conception, writing in 1906: ' . . . the notion that under the Tsarist régime prior to the revolution the working class standard of living was that of paupers is much exaggerated. On the contrary the layer of workers in large industries and big cities which was most effective and active in the economic and political struggle enjoyed a standard of living hardly lower than the corresponding layer of the German proletariat; indeed, in some trades the same, or here and there, an even higher wage, obtained in Russia than in Germany. Also in regard to working hours the difference between large industrial concerns in the two countries is scarcely significant. Hence the conception that assumes that the Russian working class has the material and cultural conditions of helots is invented out of thin air. This conception contradicts the facts of the revolution itself and the prominent role of the proletariat in it. Revolutions of this political and spiritual maturity are not made by paupers; the industrial worker in the vanguard of the struggle at Petersburg, Warsaw, Moscow, Odessa, is much closer culturally and spiritually to the West European type than is imagined by those who think that the only and indispensable school for the proletariat is bourgeois parliamentarism and 'correct' union practice.' (*AR,* I, pp. 211-212.)

Incidentally, empty stomachs, besides encouraging rebellion, lead also to submission.

Basing herself on the class struggle of the working class, whether latent or open, whether aimed at winning concessions from the capitalist class or at its overthrow, Rosa Luxemburg supported the struggle for social reforms as well as social revolution, considering the former above all a school for the latter, whose greater historical import she made clear in analysing the mutual relations of the two.

'Legislative reform and revolution are not different methods of historic development that can be picked out at pleasure from the counter of history, just as one chooses hot or cold sausages. Legislative reform and revolution are different factors in the development of class society. They condition and complement each other, and are at the same time reciprocally exclusive, as are the north and south poles, the bourgeoisie and the proletariat.

'Every legal constitution is the product of a revolution. In the history of classes, revolution is the act of political creation, while legislation is the political expression of the life of a society that has already come into being. Work for reform does not contain its own force, independent from revolution. During every historic period, work of reforms is carried on only in the direction given to it by the impetus of the last revolution, and continues as long as the impulsion of the last revolution continues to make itself felt. Or, to put it more concretely, in each historic period work for reforms is carried on only in the framework of the social form created by the last revolution. Here is the kernel of the problem.

'It is contrary to history to represent work for reforms as a long-drawn-out revolution and revolution as a condensed series of reforms. A social transformation and a legislative reform do not differ according to their duration but according to their content. The secret of historic change through the utilization of political power resides precisely in the transformation of simple quantitative modification into a new quality, or, to speak more concretely, in the passage of an historic period from one given form of society to another.

'That is why people who pronounce themselves in favour of the method of legislative reform in place of and in contradistinction to the conquest of political power and social revolution do not really choose a more tranquil, calmer and slower road to the same goal, but a different goal. Instead of a stand for the establishment of a new society they take a stand for surface modifications of the old society. If we follow the political conceptions of revisionism, we arrive at the same conclusion that is reached when we follow the economic theories of revisionism. Our program becomes not the realization of socialism, but the reform of capitalism; not the suppression of the system of wage labour, but the diminution of exploitation, that is, the suppression of the abuses of capitalism instead of the suppression of capitalism itself.' (*RR*, pp. 58-9.)

Mass Strikes and Revolution

In May, 1891, a mass strike of some 125,000 Belgian workers demanded changes in the electoral system. In April, 1893, another strike, embracing about a quarter of a million workers, broke out for a similar demand. The outcome was universal, but unequal, franchise, the votes of the rich and 'cultured' counting for two or three times those of workers and peasants. The workers, dissatisfied, carried out another mass strike nine years later, demanding a complete revision of the Constitution. These mass political strikes made a great impression on Rosa Luxemburg. Two articles devoted to the subject ('The Belgian Experiment,' *NZ*, 26 April, 1902, and 'Yet a Third Time on the Belgian Experiment,' *NZ*, 14 May, 1902) point out the revolutionary nature of the mass political strike as the specific working-class weapon of struggle. For Rosa Luxemburg the mass strikes, political and economic, constitute a central factor in the revolutionary struggle for workers' power.

Rosa Luxemburg's enthusiasm for this method and incisive understanding of it reach a new height with the Russian revolution of 1905: 'In former bourgeois revolutions where, on the one hand, the political education and leadership of the revolutionary masses was undertaken by the bourgeois parties, and on the other hand the revolutionary task was limited to the overthrow of the government, the short battle on the barricades was the appropriate form of revolutionary struggle. Today, at a time that the working class must educate, organise and lead itself in the course of the revolutionary struggle, when the revolution itself is directed not only against the established State power but also against capitalist exploitation, mass strikes appear as the natural method to mobilise the broadest proletarian layers into action, to revolutionise and organise them. Simultaneously it is a method by means of which to undermine and overthrow the established State power as well as to curb capitalist exploitation . . . In order that the working class may participate **en masse** in any direct political action, it must first organise itself, which above all means that it must obliterate the boundaries between factories and workshops, mines and foundries, it must overcome the split between workshops which the daily yoke of capitalism condemns it to. Therefore the mass strike is the first natural spontaneous form of every great revolutionary proletarian action. The more industry becomes the prevalent form of the economy, the more prominent the role of the working class, and the more developed the conflict between labour and capital, the more powerful and decisive become the mass strikes. The earlier main form of bourgeois revolutions, the battle on the barricades, the open encounter with the armed State power, is a peripheral aspect of the revolution today, only one moment in the whole process of the mass struggle of the proletariat.' (*AR*, I, pp. 227-8.)

Budapest, 1956!

Contrary to all reformists who see a Chinese wall between partial struggles for economic reform and the political struggle for revolution, Rosa Luxemburg pointed out that in a revolutionary period the economic struggle grows into a political one, and vice versa.

'The movement does not go only in one direction, from an economic to a political struggle, but also in the opposite direction. Every important political mass action, after reaching its peak, results in a series of economic mass strikes. And this rule applies not only to the individual mass strike, but to the revolution as a whole. With the spread, clarification and intensification of the political struggle not only does the economic struggle not recede, but on the contrary it spreads and at the same time becomes more organised and intensified. There exists a reciprocal influence between the two struggles. Every fresh attack and victory of the political struggle has a powerful impact on the economic struggle, in that at the same time as it widens the scope for the workers to improve their conditions and strengthens their impulse to do so, it enhances their fighting spirit. After every soaring wave of political action, there remains a fertile sediment from which sprout a thousand economic struggles. And the reverse also applies. The workers' constant economic struggle against capital sustains them at every pause in the political battle. The economic struggle constitutes, so to speak, the permanent reservoir of working class strength from which political struggles always imbibe new strength. The untiring economic fight of the proletariat leads every moment to sharp isolated conflicts here and there from which explode unforeseen political struggles on an immense scale.

'In a word, the economic struggle is the factor that advances the movement from one political focal point to another. The political struggle periodically fertilises the ground for the economic struggle. Cause and effect interchange every second. Thus we find that the two elements, the economic and political, do not incline to separate themselves from one another during the period of the mass strikes in Russia, not to speak of negating one another, as pedantic schemes would suggest.' (*AR*, pp. 201-2.)

The logical and necessary climax of the mass strike is the 'open uprising which can only be realised as the culmination of a series of partial uprisings which prepare the ground, and therefore are liable to end for a time in what looks like partial 'defeats', each of which may seem to be 'premature'.' (*AR*, p. 274.)

And what a rise in class consciousness results from the mass strikes: 'The most precious thing, because it is the most enduring, in the sharp ebb and flow of the revolutionary wave, is the proletariat's spiritual growth. The advance by leaps and bounds of the intellectual stature of the proletariat affords an inviolable guarantee of its further progress in the inevitable economic and political struggles ahead.' (*AR*, p. 187.)

And what idealism workers rise to! They put aside thoughts of whether they have the wherewithal to support themselves and their families during the struggle. They do not ask whether all the preliminary technical preparations have been made: 'Once a really serious period of mass strikes opens up, all such 'costing operations' are something like an attempt to measure the ocean with a bucket. And it is an ocean, a sea of terrible troubles and privations for the proletariat—that is the invariable cost of every revolution. The solution which a revolutionary period brings with it for this apparently insoluble problem of providing material support for the strikers, is to generate such a tremendous volume of idealism among the masses that they appear to become almost immune to the most terrible privations.' (*GW*, III, p. 457.)

It was this glimpse of the magnificent revolutionary initiative and self-sacrifice that the workers rise to during a revolution that justified Rosa's faith.

The Fight against Imperialism and War

During the two decades preceding the outbreak of the First World War support for imperialism grew steadily, within the Socialist International.

The Stuttgart Congress of the International in 1907 showed this clearly. The colonial question was placed on the agenda because at this time the jostling of imperialist powers in Africa and Asia was becoming fierce. The socialist parties did indeed speak out against the rapacity of their own governments, but as the discussion at the Stuttgart Congress showed, a consistent anti-colonialist position was far from the thoughts of many leaders of the International. The Congress appointed a Colonial Commission, the majority of which drafted a report stating that colonialism had some positive aspects. Its draft resolution stated: '(The Congress) does not reject on principle and for all time every colonial policy.' Socialists should condemn the excesses of colonialism, but should not renounce it altogether. Instead 'they are to advocate reforms, to improve the lot of the natives . . . and they are to educate them for independence by all possible means.

'To this purpose the representatives of the socialist parties should propose to their governments to conclude an international treaty, to create a Colonial Law, which shall protect the rights of the natives and which would be guaranteed by all the signatory States.'

This draft resolution was in fact defeated, but by a rather slim majority—127 against 108. Thus practically half the Congress sided openly with imperialism.

When the First World War, which was essentially a fight between the imperialist powers for the division of the colonies, broke out in 1914, its support by the majority leaders of the Socialist International did not come out of the blue.

At the Stuttgart Congress Rosa Luxemburg came out clearly against imperialism, proposing a resolution which outlined the policy necessary to meet the threat of imperialist war. 'In the event of a threat of war it is the duty of the workers and their parliamentary represent-atives in the countries involved to do everything possible to prevent the outbreak of war by taking suitable measures, which can of course change or be intensified in accordance with the intensification of the class struggle and the general political situation.

'In the event of war breaking out nevertheless, it is their duty to take measures to bring it to an end as quickly as possible, and to utilise the economic and political crisis brought about by the war to arouse the masses of the people and accelerate the overthrow of capitalist class rule.'

This resolution made it clear that socialists should oppose imperialism and its war, and that the only way to put an end to both is through the overthrow of capitalism, of which both are the outgrowth.

This resolution was passed, but even so it was becoming more and more evident that of those leaders who were not openly supporting colonialism, many did not conceive of the fight against imperialism in revolutionary terms.

These leaders, whose main spokesman was Kautsky, adopted the view that imperialism was not a necessary outgrowth of capitalism, but an abscess which the capitalist class as a whole would more and more wish to get rid of. Kautsky's theory was that imperialism was a method of expansion supported by certain small but powerful capitalist groups (the banks and the armament kings), which was contrary to the needs of the capitalist class as a whole, as expenditure on armaments reduced available capital for investment in the country and abroad and therefore affected the majority of the capitalist class which would progressively increase its opposition to the policy of armed imperialist expansion. Echoing the same ideas, Bernstein, as late as 1911, argued confidently that the desire for peace was becoming universal and that it was out of· the question that war should break out. The armaments race, according to the Kautsky-led 'Marxist Centre' was an anomaly that could be over-come by general disarmament agreements, international arbitration courts, peace alliances, and the formation of the United States of Europe. In short, the 'Marxist Centre' relied on the powers-that-be to bring peace on earth.

Rosa Luxemburg brilliantly tore to shreds this capitalist pacifism: '. . . the belief that capitalism is possible without expansion, is the theoretical formula for a certain definite tactical tendency. This conception tends to regard the phase of imperialism not as a historical necessity, not as the final bout between capitalism and socialism, but rather as the malicious invention of a group of interested parties. It tries to persuade the bourgeoisie that imperialism and militarism are deleterious even from the standpoint of bourgeois interests, in the hope that it will then be able to isolate the alleged handful of interested parties and so form a block between the proletariat and the majority of the bourgeoisie with a view to 'curbing' imperialism, starving it out by 'partial disarmament,' and 'removing its sting.' Just as a bourgeois Liberalism in its period of decay appealed from the 'ignorant' monarchs to the 'enlightened' monarchs, now the 'Marxist Centre' proposes to appeal from the 'unreasonable' bourgeoisie to the 'reasonable' bourgeoisie with a view to dissuading it from a policy of imperialism with all its catastrophic results to a policy of international disarmament treaties; from an armed struggle for world dominance to a peaceable federation of democratic national States. The general settling of accounts between the proletariat and capitalism, the solution of the great contradiction between them, resolves itself into an idyllic compromise for the 'mitigation of imperialist contradictions between the capitalist States.' (*GW*, III, p. 481.)

How apt these words are not only for the bourgeois pacifism of Kautsky and Bernstein, but for all those who adhered to the League of Nations, the United Nations, 'collective security', or Summit talks!

Rosa Luxemburg showed that imperialism and imperialist war could not be overcome within the framework of capitalism as they grow out of the vital interests of capitalist society.

The *Guiding Principles* of the Spartakus League drawn up by Rosa Luxemburg stated: 'Imperialism, the last phase and highest development of the political rule of capitalism, is the deadly enemy of the workers of all countries . . . The struggle against imperialism is at the same time the struggle of the proletariat for political power, the decisive conflict between Capitalism and Socialism. The final aim of Socialism can be achieved only if the international proletariat fights uncompromisingly against imperialism as a whole, and takes the slogan 'war against war' as a practical guide to action, summoning up all its strength and all its capacity for self-sacrifice.' (*Dokumente*, I, pp. 280-1.)

Thus the central theme of Rosa Luxemburg's anti-imperialist policy was that the fight against war is inseparable from the fight for socialism.

With great passion Rosa Luxemburg ends her most important anti-war pamphlet, *The Crisis of Social Democracy* (better known as the

Junius Brochure, as she wrote under the pseudonym Junius): 'Imperialist bestiality has been let loose to devastate the fields of Europe, and there is one incidental accompaniment for which the 'cultured world' has neither the heart nor conscience–the mass slaughter of the European proletariat . . . It is our hope, our flesh and blood, which is falling in swathes like corn under the sickle. The finest, the most intelligent, the best-trained forces of international Socialism, the bearers of the heroic traditions of the modern working-class movement, the advanced guard of the world proletariat, the workers of Great Britain, France, Germany and Russia, are being slaughtered in masses. That is a greater crime by far than the brutish sack of Louvain or the destruction of Rheims Cathedral. It is a deadly blow against the power which holds the whole future of humanity, the only power which can save the values of the past and carry them on into a newer and better human society. Capitalism has revealed its true features; it betrays to the world that it has lost its historical justification, that its continued existence can no longer be reconciled with the progress of mankind . . .

'Deutschland, Deutschland Uber Alles! Long Live Democracy! Long Live the Tsar and Slavdom! Ten thousand blankets, guaranteed in perfect condition! A hundred thousand kilos of bacon, coffee substitutes –immediate delivery! Dividends rise and proletarians fall. And with each one sinks a fighter for the future, a soldier of the Revolution, a liberator of humanity from the yoke of capitalism, and finds a nameless grave.

'The madness will cease and the bloody product of hell come to an end only when the workers of Germany and France, of Great Britain and Russia, awaken from their frenzy, extend to each other the hand of friendship, and drown the bestial chorus of imperialist hyenas with the thunderous battle cry of the modern working-class movement: 'Workers of the World Unite!' ' (*AR*, I, pp. 391-4.)

With visionary power Rosa Luxemburg states: 'Bourgeois society faces a dilemma; either a transition to Socialism, or a return to barbarism . . . we face the choice: either the victory of imperialism and the decline of all culture, as in ancient Rome–annihilation, devastation, degeneration, a yawning graveyard; or the victory of Socialism–the victory of the international working class consciously assaulting imperialism and its method: war. This is the dilemma of world history, either–or; the die will be cast by the class-conscious proletariat.' (*AR*, p. 270.)

And we who live in the shadow of the H-bomb . . .

Party and Class

Rosa Luxemburg has been accused of mechanical materialism, a conception of historical development in which objective economic forces are independent of human will. This accusation is totally unfounded. Hardly any of the great Marxists has laid greater stress on human activity as the determinant of human destiny. She wrote: 'Men do not make history of their own free will, but they do make their own history. The proletariat is dependent in its action on the given degree of maturity in social development existing at the time, but social development does not proceed independently of and apart from the proletariat, and the proletariat is as much its cause and mainspring as it is its product and consequence. The action of the proletariat is a determining factor in history, and although we can no more jump over stages of historical development than a man can jump over his own shadow, still, we can accelerate or retard that development. The victory of the Socialist proletariat will be the result of iron historical laws, and it would depend upon a thousand steps in previous, laborious and all-too-slow development. However, it will never be fulfilled unless the material conditions brought together by the historical process are vitalised with the life-giving spark of conscious will power generated in the great masses of the people.' (*AR,* I, p. 269.)

Following the line of thought propounded by Marx and Engels, Rosa Luxemburg believed that consciousness of the aims of socialism on the part of the mass of workers is a **necessary prerequisite** for achieving socialism. The Communist Manifesto states: 'All previous historical movements were movements of minorities or in the interests of minorities. The proletarian movement is the self-conscious independent movement of the immense majority, in the interest of the immense majority.' Again Engels wrote: 'The time of . . . revolutions carried through by small conscious minorities at the head of unconscious masses, is past. Where it is a question of a complete transformation of the social organisation, the masses themselves must also be in it, must themselves already have grasped what is at stake, what they are going in for with body and soul.' (F. Engels, in 1895 introduction to Marx's *The Class Struggle in France*.)

Rosa Luxemburg wrote in similar vein: 'Without the conscious will and the conscious action of the majority of the proletariat there can be no Socialism . . .' (*AR*, II, p. 606.)

Again, the *Programme of the Communist Party of Germany (Spartakus)*, drafted by Rosa, states:

'1. The Spartakus League is not a party that wishes to succeed to power either over the working class or by means of it. The Spartakus League is merely that part of the working class most convinced of its object; it is the part that directs the broad labour movement to its historical function at every step; at every single stage of the revolution it represents the final socialist aim and in all national questions the interests of the proletarian world revolution.

'2. The Spartakus League will never assume governmental authority except through the clear unambiguous will of the vast majority of the German working class; in no other way except through its conscious concurrence with the views, aims and fighting tactics of the Spartakus League.

'The proletarian revolution can only achieve clarity and maturity going step by step along the hard path of suffering, bitter experience, through defeats and triumphs.

'The victory of the Spartakus League is not at the beginning but at the end of the revolution; it is identical with the victory of the many-millioned mass of the socialist proletariat.' (*Dokumente*, II, pp. 704-5.)

While the working class as a class must be conscious of the aims of socialism and the methods of achieving it, it still needs a revolutionary party to lead it. In every factory, on every dock and on every building site, there are more advanced workers—that is, workers more experienced in the class struggle, more independent of the influence of the capitalist class—and less advanced workers. It is up to the former to organise into a revolutionary party, and try to influence and lead the latter. As Rosa Luxemburg said: 'This mass movement of the proletariat needs the lead of an organised principled force.' (*AR*, I, p. 104.)

The revolutionary party, while conscious of its leading role, must beware of slipping into a way of thinking that the party is the fount of all correct thoughts and deeds, while the working class remains an inert mass without initiative. 'Of course through the theoretical analysis of the social conditions of struggle, Social Democracy has introduced the element of consciousness into the proletarian class struggle to an unprecedented degree; it gave the class struggle its clarity of aim; it created, for the first time, a permanent mass workers' organisation, and thus built a firm backbone for the class struggle. However, it would be catastrophically wrong for us to assume that from now on all the historical initiative of the people has passed to the hands of the Social Democratic organisation alone, and that the unorganised mass of the proletariat has turned into a formless thing, into the deadweight of history. On the contrary, the popular masses continue to be the living matter of world history, even in the presence of Social Democracy; and only if there is blood circulation between the organised nucleus and the popular masses, only if one heartbeat vitalises the two, can Social Democracy prove that it is capable of great historical deeds.' (*Leipziger Volkszeitung*, pp. 26-28, June, 1913.)

The party, in consequence, should not invent tactics out of thin air, but put it as its first duty to **learn** from the experience of the mass movement and then generalise from it. The great events of working-class history have shown the correctness of this emphasis beyond all measure of doubt. The workers of Paris in 1871 established a new form of state —a state without a standing army and bureaucracy, where all officials received the average worker's salary and were subject to recall, before Marx began to generalise about the nature and structure of a workers' state. Again, the workers of Petrograd, in 1905, established a Soviet (workers' council) independently of the Bolshevik Party, actually in opposition to the local Bolshevik leadership and in face of at least suspicion, if not animosity, on the part of Lenin himself. Therefore one cannot but agree with Rosa Luxemburg when she wrote in 1904: 'The main characteristics of the tactics of struggle of Social Democracy are not 'invented,' but are the result of a continuous series of great creative acts of the elementary class struggle. Here also the unconscious precedes the conscious, the logic of the objective historical process comes before the subjective logic of its bearer.' (*NZ*, 1904, p. 491.)

It is not through didactic teaching by the party leaders that the workers learn. As Rosa Luxemburg countered to Kautsky and company: 'They think that to educate the proletarian masses in a socialist spirit means the following: to lecture to them, distribute leaflets and pamphlets among them. But no! The Socialist proletarian school does not need all this. Activity itself educates the masses.' (Rosa Luxemburg's *Speech to the Foundation Congress of the German Communist Party*.)

Finally, Rosa Luxemburg comes to this conclusion: 'Mistakes committed by a genuine revolutionary labour movement are much more fruitful and worthwhile historically than the infallibility of the very best Central Committee ' (*NZ*, 1904, p. 535.)

Placing such emphasis (and quite rightly) on the creative power of the working class, Rosa Luxemburg nonetheless inclined to under-estimate the retarding, damaging effect that a conservative organisation may have on the mass struggle. She believed that the upsurge of the masses would sweep aside such a leadership without the movement itself suffering serious damage. She wrote in 1906: 'If, at any time and under any circumstances, Germany were to experience big political struggles, an era of tremendous economic struggles would at the same time open up. Events would not stop for a second in order to ask the union leaders whether they had given their blessing to the movement or not. If they stood aside from the movement or opposed it, the result of such behaviour would be only this: the union or Party leaders would be swept away by the wave of events and the economic as well as the political struggles would be fought to a conclusion without them.' (*AR*, I, pp. 235-236.)

And it was this theme that Rosa Luxemburg reiterated again and again.

To understand the roots of Rosa Luxemburg's possible under-estimation of the role of organisation and possible overestimation of the role of spontaneity, one must look at the situation in which she worked. First of all she had to fight the opportunist leadership of the German Social Democratic Party. This leadership emphasised the factor of organisation out of all proportion, and made little of the spontaneity of the masses. Even where they accepted the possibility of a mass strike, for instance, the reformist leadership reasoned as follows: the conditions in which the mass political strike will be launched and the appropriate time—as, for instance, when the union treasuries were full—would be determined by the party and trade union leadership alone, and the date fixed by them. It was their task also to determinate the aims of the strike, which, according to Bebel, Kautsky, Hilferding, Bernstein and others, were to achieve the franchise or defend parliament. Above all, this precept must remain inviolable: that nothing is done by the workers except by order of the party and its leadership. It was with this idea of the mighty party leadership and the puny masses, that Rosa Luxemburg joined battle. But in doing so she may have bent the stick a little too far.

Another wing of the labour movement with which Rosa Luxemburg had to contend was the Polish Socialist Party (PPS). The

PPS was a chauvinistic organisation, its avowed aim the national independence of Poland. But there was no mass social basis for its struggle: the landlords and bourgeoisie stood aside from the national struggle while the Polish working class (looking upon the Russian workers as their allies) had no desire to fight for a national state (see below, Chapter 6, **Rosa Luxemburg and the National Question**). Under these conditions the PPS adopted adventuristic activities such as the organisation of terrorist groups and so on. Action was based not on the working class as a whole, but only on the party organisations. Here, too, the social process counted for little, the decision of the leadership for everything. Here, too (in her long struggle against PPS voluntarism) Rosa Luxemburg stressed the factor of spontaneity.

A third trend in the labour movement with which Rosa battled was Syndicalism, a mixture of anarchism (without its individualism and with a much-exaggerated emphasis on organisation) with the trade unions. The main base of this tendency was in France where it spread its roots in the soil of industrial backwardness and lack of concentration. It gained strength after the series of defeats suffered by the French labour movement in 1848 and 1871, and the betrayal of Millerand and the Jaurés party, which developed suspicion among the workers of all political activities and organisations. Syndicalism identified the general strike with social revolution, rather than looking upon it as only one important element of modern revolution. It believed that the general strike could be touched off by an order, and the overthrow of bourgeois rule would follow. It thus again emphasised and oversimplified the revolutionary factor; that is, that the voluntary and free will of the leaders, independent of the compulsion of a mass upsurge, could initiate decisive action. While renouncing this voluntarism, German reformists developed a similar trend. Where the French Syndicalists painted a caricature of the mass strike and revolution, the German opportunists, in making a laughing stock of it, threw out the whole idea of mass strikes and revolutions. At the same time as Rosa battled against the German brand of voluntarism, she fought the French edition in its Syndicalist form, showing it to be essentially a bureaucratic denial of workers' initiative and self-mobilisation.

The main reason for Rosa Luxemburg's overestimation of the factor of spontaneity and underestimation of the factor of organisation probably lies in the need, in the **immediate** struggle against reformism, for emphasis on spontaneity as the **first** step in all revolutions. From this one stage in the struggle of the working class, she generalised too widely to embrace the struggle as a whole.

Revolutions do indeed **start** as spontaneous acts without the leadership of a party. The French revolution started with the storming of the Bastille. Nobody organised this. Was there a party at the head of the people in rebellion? No. Even the future leaders of the Jacobins, for instance Robespierre, did not yet oppose the monarchy, and were not yet organised into a party. The revolution of 14 July, 1789, was a spontaneous act of the masses. The same was true of the Russian revolutions of 1905 and February, 1917. The 1905 revolution started through a bloody clash between the Tsar's army and police on the one hand and the mass of workers, men, women and children, on the other, led by the priest Gapon (who was actually an agent provocateur of the Tsar). Were the workers organised by a clear decisive leadership with a socialist policy of its own? Certainly not. Carrying icons, they came begging their beloved 'little Father'—the Tsar—to help them against their exploiters. This was the first step in a great revolution. Twelve years later, in February 1917, the masses, this time more experienced, and among whom there were a greater number of socialists than in the previous revolution, again rose spontaneously. No historian has been able to point a finger at the organiser of the February revolution, for it was simply not organised.

However, after being triggered off by a spontaneous uprising, revolutions move forward in a different manner. In France, the transition from the semi-republican government of the Gironde to the revolutionary one, which completely annihilated feudal property relations, was not carried out by unorganised masses without any party leadership, but under the decisive leadership of the Jacobin Party. Without such a party at the helm, this important step, which demanded an all-out fight against the Girondists, would have been impossible. The people of Paris could spontaneously, leaderlessly, rise up against the king, after decades of oppression. But the majority of them were too conservative, too lacking in historical experience and knowledge, to distinguish, after only two or three years of revolution, between those who wanted to drive the revolution as far as it would go and those who aimed at some compromise. The historical situation required a struggle to the bitter end against the party of compromise, the allies of yesterday. The conscious leadership of this great undertaking was supplied by the Jacobin Party which fixed the date and organised the overthrow of the Gironde on 10 August, 1792, down to the last detail. Similarly the October revolution was not a spontaneous act but was organised in practically all its important particulars, including the date, by the Bolsheviks. During the zigzags of the revolution between February and October—the June demonstration, the July days and subsequent orderly retreat, the rebuff of the rightist Kornilov putsch—the workers and soldiers came more closely under the influence and guidance of the Bolshevik Party. And such a party was essential to raise the revolution from its initial stages to its final victory.

While accepting that perhaps Rosa Luxemburg underestimated the importance of such a party, one should not say too little of the really great historical merit of Rosa Luxemburg, who in the face of prevailing reformism, emphasised the most important power that could break the conservative crust—that of workers' spontaneity. Her enduring strength lay in her complete confidence in the workers' historical initiative.

While pointing out some of the deficiencies in Rosa Luxemburg's position regarding the link between spontaneity and leadership in the revolution, one should be wary of concluding that her critics in the revolutionary movement, above all, Lenin, were at every point nearer a correct, balanced, Marxist analysis than she was.

Whereas Rosa Luxemburg had worked in an environment in which the main enemy of revolutionary socialism had been bureaucratic centralism, with the result that she had constantly stressed the elementary activity of the masses, Lenin had had to contend with the amorphousness of the labour movement in Russia, where the greatest danger lay in an underestimation of the element of organisation. Just as one cannot understand Rosa Luxemburg's views outside the conditions of the countries and labour movements in which she worked, so is it difficult to understand Lenin's position without due reference to the concrete historical conditions of the labour movement in Russia.

Lenin's conception of the relation between spontaneity and organisation were put forward in two main works: *What is to be Done?* (1902) and *One Step Forward, Two Steps Backward* (1904). At the time they were written, the Russian labour movement could not be compared in strength with that of Western Europe, especially Germany. It was made up of isolated, small, more or less autonomous groups, without any commonly agreed policies, and only marginally under the influence of the leading Marxists abroad, Plekhanov, Lenin, Martov, Trotsky. In these groups, because of weakness and isolation, sights were set low. While the Russian workers were rising to a high level of militancy in mass strikes and demonstrations the socialist groups propounded no more than immediately realisable economic demands; this so-called 'economist' tendency was predominant in the the the socialist groups. Lenin's *What is to be Done?* was a merciless attack on 'economism' or pure trade unionism. He argued that the spontaneity of the masses' struggle—everywhere so obvious in Russia at the time—must be supplemented by the consciousness and organisation of a party. A national party with a central newspaper of its own must be created in order to unify the local groupings and infuse the labour movement with **political** consciousness. Socialist theory must be brought to the working class from the outside; this was the only way the labour movement could move directly to the struggle for socialism. The projected party would be made up largely of professional revolutionaries, working under an extremely centralised leadership. The political leadership of the party should be the editorial board of the central newspaper. This should have the power to organise or reorganise party branches inside the country, admit or expel members and appoint local committees. Criticising the Mensheviks, Lenin wrote in 1904: 'The basic idea of comrade Martov . . . is precisely false 'democratism', the idea of the construction of the Party from the bottom to the top. My idea, on the contrary, is 'bureaucratic' in the sense that the Party should be constructed from above down to the bottom, from the Congress to the individual Party organisation.' (Lenin, *Works,* Russian, VII, pp. 365-366.)

How often have Stalinists, and many so-called non-Stalinists, the many who came after Lenin, quoted *What is to be Done?* and *One Step Forward, Two Steps Backward*, as being applicable **in toto**, in all countries and movements, whatever the stage of development!

Lenin was far from these so-called Leninists. As early as 1903, at the Second Congress of the Russian Social-Democratic Party, he pointed out some exaggerations of the formulations in *What is to be Done?*: 'The economists bent the stick to one side. In order to straighten it out again, it had to be bent towards the other side and that is what I did.' (*Works,* VI, p. 21.) Two years later, in a draft resolution written for the Third Congress, Lenin emphasised that his organisational views were not universally applicable: 'Under free political conditions our party can and will be built up entirely upon the principle of electibility. Under absolutism this is unrealisable . . . ' During the 1905 revolution, with the tremendous increase in party membership, Lenin ceased to talk of professional revolutionaries. The party was no more to be an elite organisation: 'At the Third Congress I expressed the wish that in the party committees there should be two intellectuals for every eight workers. How obsolete is this wish. Now it would be desirable that in the new party organisations, for every intellectual belonging to the Social Democracy, there should be a few hundred Social-Democratic workers.'

Whereas in *What is to be Done?* Lenin wrote that the workers through their own efforts could only reach trade union consciousness, now he wrote: 'The working class is instinctively, spontaneously Social-Democratic.' (*Works,* VIII, p. 37, quoted in R. Dunayevskaya *Marxism and Freedom*, New York, 1958, p. 182.) 'The special condition of the proletariat in capitalistic society leads to a striving of workers for socialism; a union of them with the Socialist Party bursts forth with spontaneous force in the very early stages of the movement.' Where, in 1902, Lenin wanted the party to be a tight, closely-knit, small group with very exclusive standards of membership, in 1905 he wrote that workers should be incorporated 'into the ranks of the Party organisations by the hundreds of thousands.' Again, in 1907, in a foreword to the collection, *Twelve Years*, Lenin said: 'The basic mistake of those who polemicize against *What is to be Done?* today, is that they tear this work out of the context of a definite historical milieu, a definite, now already long past period of development of our Party . . . *What is to be Done?* polemically corrected Economism, and it is false to consider the contents of the pamphlet outside of its connection with this task.' (Lenin, *Works,* Russian, XIII, p. 85.) Unwilling for *What is to be Done?* to be misused, Lenin did not relish its proposed translation in 1921 into non-Russian languages. He told Max Levien, 'that is not desirable; the translation must at least be issued with good commentaries which would have to be written by a Russian comrade very well acquainted with the history of the Communist Party of Russia in order to avoid false application.'*

When the Communist International was discussing its statutes, Lenin argued against those that were being proposed because, he said, they were 'too Russian' and overemphasised centralisation, even though these statutes did provide for freedom of criticism within the parties and for the control of the party leadership from below. Overcentralisation, Lenin argued, did not suit the conditions of Western Europe. (It is true that in Lenin's own party at the time the organisation was highly centralised, even semi-military, but this form was forced upon it by the dire conditions of the civil war.)

Lenin's views on organisation, his bending of the stick too far over to centralism, must be considered against the background of conditions in Russia.

In backward Tsarist Russia, where the working class was a small minority, the idea that the working class alone can liberate itself could easily be passed over. The more easily still, since Russia had quite a long tradition of minority organisations trying to substitute for elementary mass activity. In France it was the people who overthrew the monarchy and feudalism; in Russia, Decembrists and Narodnik terrorists took it

* Actually this pamphlet was translated into many languages without the commentary Lenin considered necessary.

RL–D

upon themselves to do this.*

Marx's statement about the democratic nature of the socialist movement, quoted previously, and Lenin's, that revolutionary Social Democracy represents 'the Jacobins indissolubly connected with the **organisation** of the proletariat' are definitely contradictory. A conscious, organised minority at the head of an unorganised mass of the people suits the bourgeois revolution, which is, after all, a revolution in the interests of the minority. But the separation of conscious minority from unconscious majority, the separation of mental and manual labour, the existence of manager and foreman on the one hand and a mass of obedient labourers on the other, may be grafted on to 'socialism' only by killing the very essence of socialism, which is the collective control of the workers over their destiny.

It is only by juxtaposing Luxemburg's and Lenin's conceptions that one can attempt to assess the historical limitations of each which were, inevitably, fashioned by the special environment in which each worked.

Emphatic as she was that the liberation of the working class can be carried out only by the working class itself, Rosa Luxemburg was impatient of all sectarian tendencies, which expressed themselves in breakaways from the mass movement and mass organisations.

Although for years at loggerheads with the majority leadership of the German Social Democratic Party, she continued to insist that it was the duty of revolutionary socialists to remain in this organisation. Even after the SPD rallied to the side of the imperialist war, after Karl Liebknecht's expulsion from the SPD parliamentary group (12 January, 1916), she and Liebknecht continued to adhere to the party on the grounds that breaking away would turn a revolutionary group into a sect. She held to this viewpoint not only when she was the leader of a tiny, insignificant revolutionary group. On the contrary, she persevered with this view when the Spartakus League gained influence and was becoming a recognisable force, as the war dragged on.

As we have seen, on 2 December, 1914, only one deputy, Liebknecht, voted against the war credits. In March, 1915, a second, Otto Rühle, joined him. In June, 1915, a thousand party office-bearers signed a manifesto opposing the class collaboration policies, and in December, 1915, as many as twenty deputies voted against the war credits in the Reichstag. In March, 1916, the SPD parliamentary group

---

* It was no accident that the Russian Social Revolutionaries, future enemies of Bolshevism, warmly approved Lenin's conception of party organisation. (I. Deutscher, *The Prophet Armed*, London, 1954, p. 94n.)

expelled the growing opposition from its midst, although it did not have the power to expel it from the party.

What happened in parliament was a reflection of what was taking place outside, in the factories, the streets, the party branches and the Socialist Youth organisation.

The anti-war journal, *Die Internationale,* edited by Rosa Luxemburg and Franz Mehring, distributed 5,000 of its one and only issue in one day (it was immediately suppressed by the police). (*Dokumente,* II, p. 135.) The Socialist Youth, at a secret conference at Easter, 1916, declared itself overwhelmingly behind Spartakus. On May Day, 1916, some 10,000 workers assembled on the Potsdamer Platz in Berlin in an anti-war demonstration. In other towns, Dresden, Jena, Hanau, anti-war demonstrations also took place. On 28 June, 1916, the day on which Liebknecht was sentenced to two and a half years' hard labour, 55,000 workers went on strike in Berlin munitions factories in solidarity with him. Demonstrations and strikes took place the same day in Stuttgart, Bremen, Braunschweig and other cities. Under the influence of the Russian revolution, in April, 1917, a huge wave of munitions strikes spread throughout the country: 300,000 workers were out in Berlin alone. Another wave of strikes of munitions workers in January/February, 1918, engulfed as many as 1½ million workers.

These strikes were largely political in nature. The Berlin strike of some ½ million workers demanded immediate peace without annexations and reparations and the right of self-determination of nations; it raised as its central slogan the revolutionary cry: 'Peace, freedom, bread.' Six workers were killed during the strike, and many wounded. Thousands of strikers were conscripted into the army.

Against this background Rosa Luxemburg continued to argue for remaining in the SPD right up to April, 1917, when the Centre, led by Kautsky, Bernstein and Hasse, split from the Right and formed a new party—the Independent Social-Democratic Party (USPD). The USPD was a purely parliamentary party which did not want to stir the workers up into mass strikes and demonstrations against the war, but aimed to put pressure on the governments of the belligerent countries to negotiate peace. Spartakus League, formed in January, 1916, as a faction inside the SPD, now attached itself loosely to the USPD, keeping its separate organisation and its right of independent action. Only after the outbreak of the German revolution on 29 December, 1918, did the League finally sever its connections with the USPD and establish an independent party —the Communist Party of Germany (Spartakus).

There had been constant pressure from the ranks of the revolutionaries to leave the SPD and later the USPD. But Rosa Luxemburg resisted this. There had been a precedent for breaking away in 1891, when quite a large group of revolutionaries split from the SPD, accusing it of reformism, and founded an Independent Socialist Party. This had enjoyed a very short life before completely disappearing.

On 6 January, 1917, Rosa Luxemburg put the case against those revolutionaries who wished to split from the SPD:

'However commendable and comprehensible the impatience and bitterness which leads so many of the best elements to leave the party today, a flight remains a flight. It is a betrayal of the masses, who, sold to the bourgeoisie, writhe and choke from the stranglehold of Scheidemann and Legien. One may withdraw from small sects when they do not suit one any longer in order to found new sects. It is nothing more than immature fantasy to want to liberate the mass of the proletariat from this heavy and terrible yoke of the bourgeoisie by a simple withdrawal, and thus set a brave example. The discarding of membership cards as an illusion of liberation, is nothing but the illusion, stood on its head, that power is inherent in a membership card. Both are different poles of organisational cretinism, the constitutional sickness of old German Social-Democracy. The collapse of German Social-Democracy is an historical process of immense dimensions, a general struggle between the working class and the bourgeoisie, and one should not run from this battlefield in order to breathe purer air behind a protective bush. This battle of giants should be fought to the end. The fight against the deadly stranglehold of offical Social-Democracy, and the official Free Trade Unions, which was imposed by the ruling class upon the neck of the misled and betrayed working class, should be fought with all force to the end. We should stand by the masses to the end, even in the most terrible struggle. The liquidation of this 'heap of organised corruption,' which today calls itself Social Democracy, is not the private affair of the few, or of a few groups . . . The decisive fate of the class struggle in Germany for decades is the fight against the authorities of Social Democracy and the trade unions, and therefore these words apply to each of us to the very end: 'Here I stand, I can do nothing else'.' (*Dokumente II,* p. 525.)

Rosa Luxemburg's opposition to leaving the mass workers' party did not cover any concession to reformism. Thus at a conference of Spartakus on 7 January, 1917, the following resolution inspired by her was passed: 'The Opposition stays in the Party in order to thwart and fight the policy of the majority at every step, to defend the masses from an imperialist policy covered over with the mantle of Social-Democracy, and to use the Party as a field of recruitment for the proletarian, anti-militarist class struggle.' (*Dokumente II,* p. 528.)

Rosa Luxemburg's reluctance to form an independent revolutionary party followed her slowness to react to changed circumstances. It was a central factor in the belatedness of building a revolutionary party in Germany. In this, however, she was not alone. Lenin was no quicker to break with Kautsky than Rosa. There is no ground to the Stalinist story according to which Lenin was opposed to the revolutionary Left's adherence to the SPD and continuing association with Kautsky.* Actually, Rosa Luxemburg made a clearer assessment of Kautsky and co. and broke with them long before Lenin did. For some two decades Lenin looked upon Kautsky as the greatest living Marxist. A few instances: *What is to be Done?* quotes Kautsky as the main authority for its central theme, and praises the German Social-Democratic Party as a model for the Russian movement. In December, 1906, Lenin wrote: 'The vanguard of the Russian working class knows Karl Kautsky for some time now as its writer'; he described Kautsky as 'the leader of the German revolutionary Social Democrats.' (Lenin, *Works,* XI, p. 330.) In August, 1908, he cited Kautsky as his authority on questions of war and militarism. (*Works,* XV, pp. 173-176.) In 1910, at the time of Rosa Luxemburg's debate with Kautsky on the question of the path to power, Lenin sided with him against her. And as late as February, 1914, Lenin invoked Kautsky as a Marxist authority in his dispute with Rosa Luxemburg on the national question. Only the outbreak of the war and the betrayal of internationalism by Kautsky shattered Lenin's illusions in him. Then he admitted: 'Rosa Luxemburg was right; she realised long ago that Kautsky was a time-serving theorist, serving the majority of the Party, in short, serving opportunism.' (*Letter to Shliapnikov,* 27 October, 1914.)

The form of organisation of the socialist workers' movement everywhere and at every stage of development of the struggle for power has an important influence on the moulding of workers' power itself. Hence a debate on the form of organisation of the revolutionary party has an importance that goes beyond the stage in which a certain accepted form of organisation is being applied. In no country did the debate on organisational problems assume as sharp a tone as in the Russian labour movement. Much of this was due to the vast distance between the final aim of the movement and the autocratic semi-feudal reality in which it arose, a reality that prevented a free organisation of workers.

Where Rosa Luxemburg's position regarding the relation between

---

* See, for instance, J. V. Stalin, 'Some Questions Concerning the History of Bolshevism', *Works,* Vol. XIII, pp. 86-104; *Dokumente,* Vol. II, especially the preface: F. Oelssner, *Rosa Luxemburg,* Berlin, 1956.

spontaneity and organisation was a reflection of the immediate needs facing revolutionaries in a labour movement controlled by a conservative bureaucracy, Lenin's original position—that of 1902-4—was a reflection of the amorphousness of a vital, fighting revolutionary movement at the first stage of its development under a backward, semi-feudal and autocratic regime.

However, whatever the historical circumstances moulding Rosa's thoughts regarding organisation, these thoughts showed a great weakness in the German revolution of 1918-19.

Rosa Luxemburg and the National Question

Rosa Luxemburg, as leader of a workers' party in Poland, a country divided among three empires—Russian, German and Austrian—had necessarily to take a definite position on the national question. She held to this position from its formulation in 1896 in her first scientific research work, *The Industrial Development of Poland*, till the end of her life, despite sharp conflicts with Lenin on the subject.

Her attitude was both a continuation of and diversion from the teachings of Marx and Engels on the national question, and in order to understand it properly it is necessary to glance—even if cursorily—at their attitude to the question.

Marx and Engels lived during the rise of capitalism in Europe, a period of bourgeois democratic revolutions. The framework of a bourgeois democracy was the national state, and the duty of socialists, according to them, was to fight 'in alliance with the bourgeoisie against absolute monarchy, against feudal land-ownership and the petty bourgeoisie.' (*The Communist Manifesto*.) The greatest enemy of all democratic revolutions, they stated in 1848, was Tsarist Russia, and second only to it, Hapsburg Austria. Russia, the enslaver of Poland, was the chief butcher of the Kossuth democratic revolution in Hungary (1849); Russia and Austria together, through direct and indirect intervention in the internal affairs of the Germans and Italians, prevented the complete unification of these nations. Marx and Engels consequently supported all national movements which were directed against the Tsars and Hapsburgs. At the same time, using the same criterion, they opposed national movements which objectively played into the hands of the Tsars or the Hapsburgs.

The independence of Poland would have had tremendous revolutionary repercussions, argued Marx and Engels. Firstly, a wall would be created between democratic revolutionary Western and Central Europe and the 'gendarme of Europe', Russia. Secondly, the Hapsburg Empire, shaken as it would be by a national uprising of the Poles, would collapse following national uprisings of other nations; all the nations of this empire would then be free, and the Austrian Germans would be able to unite with the rest of Germany; this would constitute the most consistent democratic revolutionary solution to the German question. Thirdly, the independence of Poland would strike a sharp blow against the Prussian Junkers, thus further strengthening democratic revolutionary tendencies in Germany as a whole.

Marx and Engels called on all democratic movements in Europe to wage war on Tsarist Russia, the chief enemy of all progress. Specifically they called on revolutionary Germany to take up arms for the emancipation of Poland. A democratic war against Tsarism would safeguard the national independence of Poland and Germany, hasten the downfall of absolutism in Russia and give a fillip to the revolutionary forces throughout Europe.

Marx and Engels, while supporting the Polish and Hungarian (Magyar) national movements, did not support others. Thus, for instance, during the 1848 revolution, they condemned the national movements of the South Slavs–Croats, Serbs, and Czechs. They did this because they thought that these movements objectively aided the main enemy: Croatian troops, who hated the Magyars more than they did the Hapsburg Empire, helped the Tsar's troops as they marched into Hungary; Czech troops helped to suppress revolutionary Vienna.

In all wars in which Tsarist Russia was involved, Marx and Engels did not adopt a position of neutrality or opposition to both contending camps, but one of militant opposition to Russia alone. Thus they criticised the British and French governments during the Crimean War for not waging war consistently to the bitter end against Russia. In the Russo-Turkish War that broke out in 1877, Marx again supported 'the gallant Turks' (*Letter to Sorge,* 27 September, 1877, *Marx-Engels Correspondence,* London, 1941, pp. 348-349.) To the end of their lives Tsarist Russia represented for Marx and Engels the main bastion of reaction and war against her was a revolutionary duty.

Because of the criterion they used to judge national movements–their effect on the bourgeois democratic revolution in West and Central Europe–Marx and Engels naturally limited their conclusions regarding national questions to Europe (and North America) where capitalist development was more or less advanced. They did not, justifiably at that time, attribute the concept of revolutionary bourgeois nationalism to Asian, African or South American countries. Thus for instance, Engels wrote: 'In my opinion the colonies proper, i.e. the countries occupied by a European population, Canada, the Cape, Australia, will all become independent; on the other hand the countries inhabited by a native population, which are simply subjugated, India, Algiers, and the Dutch, Portuguese and Spanish possessions, must be taken over for the time being by the proletariat and led as rapidly as possible towards independence.' (*Correspondence*, p. 399.) Engels thought it possible that India might emancipate itself through a revolution, but such an event would have only secondary importance for Europe. If India should liberate itself, 'this will have to be given full scope . . . as the proletariat emancipating itself cannot conduct any colonial wars.' But the idea that the emancipation of the colonies could precede the socialist revolutions in Europe, or even aid them considerably, was completely foreign to Engels (as to Marx). If India, Algeria or Egypt should free themselves, then this 'would certainly be the best thing for us. We shall have enough to do at home. Once Europe is reorganised, and North America, that will furnish such colossal power and such an example that the semi-civilised countries will follow in their wake of their own accord.' (*Correspondence.*)

Rosa Luxemburg, in the footsteps of Marx and Engels, considered the national movement mainly European, attributing only small importance to the Asian and African national movements. Like Marx and Engels, she also rejected any absolute criterion for judging struggles for national independence. She was, however, no follower who merely repeated the words of the founders of scientific socialism.

Quite early in her political life, she pointed out that the situation in Europe in general, and Russia in particular, had changed so much towards the end of the nineteenth century, that the position of Marx and Engels towards national movements in Europe had become untenable.

In Western and Central Europe the period of bourgeois democratic revolutions had passed. The Prussian Junkers had managed to establish their rule so firmly that they were no more in need of aid from the Tsar. At the same time Tsarist rule ceased to be the impregnable bastion of reaction, deep cracks beginning to cleave its walls: the mass strikes of workers in Warsaw, Lodz, Petrograd, Moscow and elsewhere in the Russian Empire; the rebellious awakening of the peasants. Actually, whereas at the time of Marx and Engels the centre of revolution was in Western and Central Europe, now, towards the end of the nineteenth century and at the beginning of the twentieth, it had passed east to

Russia. Whereas at the time of Marx Tsarism was the main gendarme suppressing revolutionary uprisings elsewhere, now Tsarism itself came to need the help (mainly financial) of the Western capitalist powers. Instead of Russian bullets and roubles going westwards, now German, French, British and Belgian munitions and marks, francs and pounds flowed in a widening stream to Russia. Rosa Luxemburg pointed out further, that basic changes had taken place as regards the national aspirations of her motherland, Poland. Whereas at the time of Marx and Engels the Polish nobles were leaders of the national movement, now, with the increasing capitalist developments of the country, they were losing ground socially, and turning to Tsarism as an ally in the suppression of progressive movements in Poland. The result was that the Polish nobility cooled to aspirations toward national independence. The Polish bourgeoisie also became antagonistic to the desire for national independence, as it found the main markets for its industry in Russia. 'Poland is bound to Russia with chains of gold,' Rosa Luxemburg said. 'Not the national state but the state of rapine, corresponds to capitalist development.' (*Przeglad Socjaldemokratyczny,* theoretical organ of the SDKPL, 1908, No. 6.) The Polish working class, too, according to Rosa Luxemburg, was not interested in the separation of Poland from Russia, as they saw in Moscow and Petrograd the allies of Warsaw and Lodz. Hence there were no social forces of any weight in Poland interested in fighting for national independence. Only the intelligentsia still cherished the idea, but they by themselves represented a small social force. Rosa Luxemburg concluded her analysis of the social forces in Poland and their attitude to the national question with the following words: 'The recognisable direction of social development has made it clear to me that there is no social class in Poland that has at one and the same time both an interest in and ability to achieve the restoration of Poland.' (*NZ,* 1895-6, p. 466.)

From this analysis she came to the conclusion that under capitalism the slogan of national independence had no progressive value, and could not be realised by the internal forces of the Polish nation; only the intervention of one or another imperialist power could bring it into being. Under socialism, argued Rosa Luxemburg, there would not be any place for the slogan of national independence, as national oppression would be no more, and the international unity of humanity will have been realised. Thus under capitalism the real independence of Poland could not be realised, and any steps in that direction would not have any progressive value, while under socialism there would be no need for such a slogan. Hence the working class had no need for the struggle for national self-determination of Poland, and this struggle was in fact reactionary. The national slogans of the working class should be limited to the demand for national autonomy in cultural life.

In taking this position, Rosa Luxemburg and her party, the SDKPL, came into bitter conflict with the right-wing members of the Polish Socialist Party (PPS) led by Pilsudski (the future military dictator of Poland). These were nationalists who paid lip service to socialism. Lacking a mass basis for their nationalism, they contrived adventures, plotting with foreign powers to the extent even of relying on a future world war as the midwife of national independence. In Galicia, the stronghold of the right-wing PPS, the Poles, under Austrian rule, received better treatment than those in the Russian Empire, mainly because the rulers of the Hapsburg Empire, a medley of nationalites, had to rely on the Polish ruling class to fortify their imperial rule. Hence the PPS leaders inclined to prefer the Hapsburg Empire to the Russian, and during the First World War they acted as recruiting agents for Vienna and Berlin. Earlier, during the 1905 revolution, Daszynski, the leader of the PPS in Galicia, had gone so far as to condemn the mass strikes of Polish workers, because, according to him, they tended to identify the struggle of the Polish workers with that of the Russian, and thus undermine the national unity of the Poles. It is only when one has a clear view of Rosa Luxemburg's opponents in the Polish labour movement that one can properly understand her position on the Polish national question.

The struggle that Rosa had to wage against the chauvinistic PPS coloured her entire attitude to the national question in general. In opposing the nationalism of the PPS she bent so far backwards that she opposed all reference to the right of self-determination in the programme of the party. It is because of this that her party, the SDKPL, split as early as 1903 from the Russian Social-Democratic Party, and never subsequently joined the Bolsheviks organisationally.

Lenin agreed with Rosa Luxemburg in her opposition to the PPS, and, with her, argued that the duty of the Polish socialists was not to fight for national independence or secession from Russia, but for international unity of the Polish and Russian workers. However, as a member of an oppressing nation, Lenin, rightly, was wary lest a nihilistic attitude to the national question should bring grist to the mill of Great Russian chauvinism. Hence, while the Polish workers could, and should, avoid demanding the establishment of the national state, Russian socialists should fight for the right of the Poles to have their separate state if they so wished: 'The great historical merit of our comrades, the Polish Social-Democrats, is that they have advanced the slogan of internationalism, that they have said: 'we treasure the fraternal alliance of the proletariat of all countries more than anything else and we shall never go to war for the liberation of Poland.' This is their great merit, and this is why we have always regarded only these Social-Democratic comrades in Poland as Socialists. The others are patriots, Polish Plekhanovs. But this unique situation, in which in order to safeguard socialism, it was found necessary to fight against rabid, morbid nationalism, has been productive of a strange phenomenon: comrades come to us and say that we must renounce the freedom of Poland, its right to secession.

'Why should we, Great Russians, who have been oppressing a greater number of nations than any other people, why should we repudiate the right of secession for Poland, the Ukraine, Finland? . . . the Polish Social-Democrats argue that precisely because they find the union with the Russian workers advantageous, they are opposed to Poland's secession. They have a perfect right to do so. But these people do not wish to understand that in order to strengthen internationalism there is no need to reiterate the same words; what we in Russia do is to stress the right of secession for the subject nations, while in Poland we must stress the right of such nations to unite. The right to unite implies the right to secede. We Russians must emphasise the right to secede, while the Poles must emphasise the right to unite.' (V. I. Lenin, *Selected Works*, V, pp. 307-308.)

The difference between Lenin and Luxemburg on the national question may be summarised as follows: While Rosa Luxemburg, proceeding from the struggle against Polish nationalism, inclined to a nihilistic attitude to the national question, Lenin saw realistically that, the positions of oppressed and oppressor nations being different, their attitude to the same question must be different. Thus, starting from different and opposing situations, they proceed in opposite directions to reach the same point of international workers' unity. Secondly, while Rosa Luxemburg disposed of the question of national self-determination as incompatible with the class struggle, Lenin subordinated it to the class struggle (in the same way as he took advantage of all other democratic strivings as weapons in the general revolutionary struggle). The fount of Lenin's approach to the national question, missing in Rosa Luxemburg, is the dialectic: he saw the unity of opposites in national oppression, and the subordination of the part —the struggle for national independence—to the whole—the international struggle for socialism.

Rosa Luxemburg's strength regarding the national question lies, as elsewhere, in her complete devotion to internationalism and her independence of thought. This led her, via Marx's method, to see how the position of Poland had changed *vis-a-vis* Russia between Marx's time and her own. It caused her, contrary to Marx, to oppose the national struggle of Poland, but at the same time, and again contrary to Marx and Engels, led her to **support** the national movement of the South Slavs against Turkey. Marx and Engels had argued that to halt the advance of Tsarism the unity of the Turkish Empire had to be defended; and the national movements of the South Slavs, which were engulfed in Pan-Slavic ideas, and were blind weapons in the hands of Tsarism, had to be opposed. Rosa Luxemburg made an excellent analysis of the new conditions in the Balkans since the time of Marx. She concluded first that the liberation of the Balkan nations suppressed by the Turks would rouse the nations of the Austro-Hungarian Empire. The end of the Turkish Empire in Europe would also mean the end of the Hapsburg Empire. Secondly, she argued that since Marx's time the national movement of the Balkans had come under the dominion of the bourgeoisie, and hence any continuation of Russian influence was due only to suppression by Turkey. The liberation of the Balkan peoples from the Turkish yoke would not enhance the influence of Tsarism but would weaken it, as these peoples would be under the leadership of a young and progressive bourgeoisie which would clash more and more with reactionary Tsarism. Thus, in the case of the Balkan nations, Rosa Luxemburg's attitude to their national strivings differed greatly from her attitude to Poland.

Rosa's lively independence of thought was tempered nevertheless by the weakness that lay, as we have seen in some of the questions already dealt with, in her tendency to generalize too readily from her immediate experiences to the labour movement elsewhere.

Rosa Luxemburg's criticism of the Bolsheviks in power

During September and October 1918, while in Breslau prison, Rosa Luxemburg wrote a pamphlet on the Russian revolution. As a basis, she used not only the German but also the Russian Press of the time that was smuggled by her friends into her prison cell. She never finished or polished the work, for the beginning of the German revolution opened the doors of her prison.

The first edition of this pamphlet was published in 1922, after Rosa Luxemburg's death, by her comrade-in-arms, Paul Levi. This edition, however, was not complete, and in 1928 a new edition was published on the basis of a newly-found manuscript.

Rosa Luxemburg was a most enthusiastic supporter of the October Revolution and the Bolshevik Party, and she made this clear in her pamphlet, writing: 'Whatever a party could offer of courage, revolutionary far-sightedness and consistency in an historic hour, Lenin, Trotsky and the other comrades have given in good measure. All the revolutionary honour and capacity which Western Social Democracy lacked, was represented by the Bolsheviks. Their October uprising was not only the actual salvation of the Russian Revolution; it was also the salvation of the honour of international socialism.' (*The Russian Revolution*, p. 16.)

Again she wrote: 'It is not a matter of this or that secondary question of tactics, but of the capacity for action of the proletariat, the strength to act, the will to power of Socialism as such. In this, Lenin and Trotsky and their friends were the **first,** those who went ahead as an example to the proletariat of the world; they are still **the only ones** up to now who can cry with Hutten: 'I have dared!'

'This is the essential and **enduring** in Bolshevik policy. In **this** sense theirs is the immortal historical service of having marched at the head of the international proletariat with the conquest of political power and the practical placing of the problems of the realisation of Socialism and of having advanced mightily the settlement of the score between Capital and Labour in the entire world ... And in **this** sense, the future everywhere belongs to 'Bolshevism.' (*Russ.*, p. 56.)

Although praising the October revolution in the highest terms, Rosa Luxemburg believed that an uncritical acceptance of everything the Bolsheviks did would not be of service to the labour movement. The Marxist method of analysis, according to her, was to accept nothing that had not been submitted first to revolutionary criticism.

It was clear to her that the conditions of isolation of the Russian revolution caused by the betrayal of Western Social Democracy must lead to distortions in its development. Without international revolutionary support, 'even the greatest energy and the greatest sacrifices of the proletariat in a single country must inevitably become tangled in a maze of contradictions and blunders.' (*Russ.*, p. 5.)

After pointing out some of these contradictions and blunders, she clearly uncovers their causes, saying: 'Everything that happens in Russia is comprehensible and represents an inevitable chain of causes and effects, the starting point and end term of which are: the failure of the German proletariat and the occupation of Russia by German imperialism. It would be demanding something superhuman from Lenin and his comrades if we should expect from them that under such circumstances they should conjure forth the finest democracy, the most exemplary dictatorship of the proletariat, and a flourishing socialist economy. By their determined revolutionary stand, their exemplary strength in action and their unbreakable loyalty to international socialism, they have contributed whatever could possibly be contributed under such devilishly hard conditions.' (*Russ.*, pp. 54-5.)

While objective factors may lead revolutions to blunder, **subjective factors** in the leadership may make these blunders dangerous. They contain a special hazard when they are turned into virtues. 'The danger begins only when they make a virtue of necessity and want to freeze into a complete theoretical system all the tactics forced upon them by these fatal circumstances, and want to recommend them to the international proletariat as a model of socialist tactics.' (*Russ.*, p. 55.)

But it was precisely this dangerous idea that was swallowed lock, stock and barrel by the Stalinist parties (and, alas, also by some who call themselves anti-Stalinist).

Rosa Luxemburg criticised the Bolsheviks in power for what she

considered their wrong policies with regard to the following:
1.   the land question.
2.   the nationalities question.
3.   the Constituent Assembly.
4.   the democratic rights of workers.
We shall deal with each problem separately.

A socialist land policy, argued Rosa Luxemburg, must aim to encourage the socialisation of agricultural production: ' . . . only the nationalisation of the large landed estates, as the technically most advanced and most concentrated means and methods of agrarian production, can serve as the point of departure for the socialist mode of production on the land. Of course, it is not necessary to take away from the small   peasant his parcel of land, and we can with confidence leave him to be won over voluntarily by the superior advantages of social production and to be persuaded of the advantages first of union in cooperatives and then finally of inclusion in the general socialised economy as a whole. Still, every socialist economic reform on the land must obviously begin with large and medium land ownership. Here the property right must first of all be turned over to the nation, or to the State, which, with a socialist government, amounts to the same thing; for it is this alone which affords the possibility of organising agricultural production in accord with the requirements of interrelated, large-scale social production.' (*Russ.*, p. 18.)

However, Bolshevik policy was quite contrary to this: '. . . the slogan launched by the Bolsheviks, immediate seizure and distribution of the land by the peasants . . . not only is . . . not a socialist measure; it even cuts off the way to such measures; it piles up insurmountable obstacles to the socialist transformation of agrarian relations.' (*Russ.*, p. 19.)

And Rosa Luxemburg, rightly and, as life proved, prophetically, pointed out that the distribution of the landed estates among the peasants would strengthen the power of private property in the country-side, and thus would heap added difficulties in the path of the socialis-ation of agriculture in the future: 'Formerly there was only a small caste of noble and capitalist landed proprietors and a small minority of rich village bourgeoisie to oppose a socialist reform on the land. And their expropriation by a revolutionary mass movement of the people is mere child's play. But now, after the 'seizure', as an opponent of any attempt at socialisation of agrarian production, there is an enormous, newly-developed and powerful mass of owning peasants who will defend their newly-won property with tooth and nail against every socialist attack.' (*Russ.*, pp. 20-21.)

And how important this fact—the isolation of a small working class in a sea of antagonistic, backward, petty capitalist peasants, proved to be in the rise of Stalin!

However, Lenin and Trotsky had no alternative. It is true that the Bolshevik Party programme provided for nationalisation of all landed estates. And for many years Lenin had argued heatedly against the Social Revolutionaries who were in favour of distributing the landlords' land among the peasants. However, in 1917, when the land problem demanded an immediate solution, he straight away adopted the slogans of the much-condemned Social Revolutionaries, or rather, of the spontaneous peasant movement. If the Bolsheviks had not done this, they, and the urban working class they led, would have been isolated from the countryside, and the revolution would have been stillborn, or at most short-lived (as was the Hungarian revolution of 1919).

By no stretch of strategy or tactics could the Bolsheviks overcome a basic contradiction in the Russian Revolution, the fact that it was carried out by two different contradictory classes, the working class and the peasantry, the former collectivist, the latter individualist. As early as in 1906 Trotsky had postulated the prospect that the future revolution, in which the working class would lead the peasants, would end with the latter so bitterly opposing the former, that only the spreading of the revolution could save the workers' power from being overthrown: 'The Russian proletariat . . . will meet with organised hostility on the part of world reaction and with readiness on the part of the world proletariat to lend the revolution organised assistance. Left to itself, the working class of Russia will inevitably be crushed by the counter-revolution at the moment when the peasantry turns its back upon the proletariat. Nothing will be left to the workers but to link the fate of their own political rule, and consequently the fate of the whole Russian Revolution, with that of the socialist revolution in Europe.' (L. Trotsky, *Itogy i Perspektivy,* Results and Perspectives, Moscow, 1919 edition, p. 80.)

Rosa Luxemburg's estimate of the Bolshevik land policy shows much true insight into the situation in the Russian Revolution, and points out the frequent dangers inherent in the Bolshevik policies. But the situation did not allow the Bolsheviks any other revolutionary land policy besides the one they implemented: acceding to the democratic, spontaneous wish of the peasants to distribute the land expropriated from the landlords.

Rosa Luxemburg was no less critical of the Bolshevik policy on the question of nationalities, warning of the gravest dangers to the revolution: 'The Bolsheviks are in part responsible for the fact that the

RL–E

military defeat was transformed into the collapse and breakdown of Russia. Moreover, the Bolsheviks themselves have, to a great extent, sharpened the objective difficulties of this situation by a slogan which they placed in the foreground of their policies: the so-called right of self-determination of peoples, or—something which was really implicit in this slogan—the disintegration of Russia.' (*Russ.*, p. 23.) Instead of the slogan of self-determination she proposed the policy of 'working for the most compact union of the revolutionary forces throughout the area of the Empire . . . of defending tooth and nail the integrity of the Russian Empire as an area of revolution and opposing to all forms of separatism the solidarity and inseparability of the proletarians in all lands within the sphere of the Russian Revolution as the highest command of politics.' (*Russ.*, p. 29.)

How wrong Rosa Luxemburg was on this question!

If the Bolsheviks had followed her advice on this issue the ruling classes of the formerly oppressed nations would have managed more and more to rally the popular masses around them and so enhance the isolation of the Soviet power. Only by the formerly oppressing nation putting forward the slogan of self-determination, could they gain the revolutionary unity of all peoples. It was in this way that the Bolsheviks did manage to rally at least part of the territory lost in the world war and the beginning of the civil war—Ukraine, for instance. It was because of a deviation from this policy of self-determination for all peoples that the Red Army was first repulsed at the gate of Warsaw, and then brought upon themselves the hatred of the Georgians by marching into and occupying Georgia in a most bureaucratic, anti-democratic fashion.*

In the case of the national question, as well as the land question, Rosa Luxemburg erred because she departed from the principle of popular decision, a principle so central to her thoughts and actions in general.

One of the criticisms Rosa Luxemburg levelled at the Bolsheviks concerned their dispersal of the Constituent Assembly. She wrote: 'It is a fact that Lenin and his comrades were stormily demanding the calling of a Constituent Assembly up to the time of their October victory, and that the policy of dragging out this matter on the part of the Kerensky government constituted an article in the indictment of that government by the Bolsheviks and was the basis of some of their most violent attacks upon it.

---

* Rosa Luxemburg's criticism of the nationalities policy of the Bolsheviks in power was a continuation of her differences with them on this issue over nearly two decades. (See Chapter 6.)

'Indeed, Trotsky says in his interesting pamphlet, *From October to Brest-Litovsk,* that the October Revolution represented 'the salvation of the Constituent Assembly' as well as the revolution as a whole. 'And when we said,' he continues, 'that the entrance to the Constituent Assembly could not be reached through the Preliminary Parliament of Zeretelli, but only through the seizure of power by the Soviets, we were entirely right'.' After thus calling for the Constituent Assembly, the same leaders dispersed it on 6 January, 1918.

What Rosa Luxemburg proposed in her pamphlet was the idea of Soviets plus Constituent Assembly. But life itself showed quite clearly that this would have led to a dual power, which would have threatened the organ of workers' power, the Soviets. The Bolshevik leaders justified the dispersal of the Constituent Assembly in the first place on the grounds that the elections had been held under an obsolete law, which gave undue weight to the rich minority of the peasants who, at the one and only session of the Assembly, refused to ratify the decrees on land, peace and the transfer of power to the Soviets. Rosa Luxemburg countered this by arguing that the Bolsheviks could simply have held new elections which did not suffer from past distortions.

But the real reason for the dispersal lay deeper than this.

It was first of all a result of the fact that while the Soviets were largely working-class organisations, the Constituent Assembly was based mainly on the votes of the peasants. It was therefore no accident that the Bolsheviks, who had the overwhelming majority in the Second Congress of the Soviets (8 November, 1917) which were elected by some 20 million people, did not command the support of more than a quarter of the Constituent Assembly elected by all the people of Russia. The peasant, devoted to private property, could not identify himself with Bolshevism, even if he was happy to have Bolshevik support for land distribution and the fight for peace. The Soviets were therefore a much more reliable support for workers' rule than the Constituent Assembly ever could be.

But there is an even more basic reason—one that has nothing to do with the peasant predominance in the Russian population—for not having a Constituent Assembly (or Parliament) side by side with Soviets. Soviets are the **specific** form of rule of the working class, in the same way as parliament was the specific form of domination of the bourgeoisie.

Actually in the German Revolution, Rosa Luxemburg radically altered her standpoint and vigorously opposed the slogan of the USPD: Workers' Councils **and** a National Assembly. Thus, on 20 November, 1918, she wrote: 'Whoever pleads for a National Assembly is consciously or unconsciously depressing the revolution to the historical level of a

bourgeois revolution; he is a camouflaged agent of the **bourgeoisie** or an unconscious representative of the petty bourgeoisie . . .

'The alternatives before us today are not democracy and dictatorship. They are **bourgeois** democracy and socialist democracy. The dictatorship of the proletariat is democracy in a socialist sense.' (*AR*, II, p. 606.)

Rosa's chief criticism of the Bolsheviks was that they were responsible for restricting and undermining workers' democracy. And on this issue the whole tragic history of Russia proves that she was, prophetically, absolutely correct.

The heart of Rosa Luxemburg's pamphlet on the Russian Revolution, as of all she wrote and said, was a belief in the workers, the conviction that they, and they alone, are capable of overcoming the crisis facing humanity. She fervently believed that workers' democracy is inseparable from proletarian revolution and socialism. She wrote: ' . . . socialist democracy is not something which begins only in the promised land after the foundations of socialist economy are created; it does not come as some sort of Christmas present for the worthy people who, in the interim, have loyally supported a handful of socialist dictators. Socialist democracy begins simultaneously with the beginnings of the destruction of class rule and of the construction of socialism. It begins at the very moment of the seizure of power by the socialist party. It is the same thing as the dictatorship of the proletariat.

'Yes, dictatorship! But this dictatorship consists in the **manner of applying democracy,** not in its **elimination,** in energetic, resolute attacks upon the well-entrenched rights and economic relationships of bourgeois society, without which a socialist transformation cannot be accomplished. But this dictatorship must be the work of the **class** and not of a little leading minority in the name of the class . . .' (*Russ.*, p. 54.)

Although she unhesitatingly supported the working-class dictatorship directed against the enemies of socialism, she argued that only complete and consistent democracy could ensure the rule of the working class and could give scope to its tremendous potentialities. She claimed that the Bolsheviks deviated from this conception: 'The tacit assumption underlying the Lenin-Trotsky theory of the dictatorship is this: that the socialist transformation is something in which a ready-made formula lies completed in the pocket of the revolutionary party, which needs only to be carried out energetically in practice. This is, unfortunately—or perhaps fortunately—not the case. Far from being a sum of ready-made prescriptions which have only to be applied, the practical realisation of socialism as an economic, social and juridical system is something which lies completely hidden in the mists of the future. What we possess in our programme is nothing but a few main signposts which indicate the general direction in which to look for the necessary measures, and the indications are mainly negative in character at that. Thus we know more or less what we must eliminate at the outset in order to free the road for a socialist economy. But when it comes to the nature of the thousand concrete, practical measures, large and small, necessary to introduce socialist principles into economy, law and all social relationships, there is no key in any socialist party programme or text book. That is not a shortcoming but rather the very thing that makes scientific socialism superior to the Utopian varieties. The socialist system of society should only be, and can only be, an historical product, born out of the school of its own experiences, born in the course of its realisation, as a result of the developments of living history, which— just like organic nature of which, in the last analysis, it forms a part —has the fine habit of always producing along with any real social need the means to its satisfaction, along with the task simultaneously the solution. However, if such is the case, then it is clear that socialism by its very nature cannot be decreed or introduced by *ukase* [edict].' (*Russ.,* pp. 45-46.)

And Rosa Luxemburg predicted that the collective of the Russian workers would not take an active part in economic and social life: ' . . . socialism will be decreed from behind a few official desks by a dozen intellectuals . . . with the repression of political life in the land as a whole, life in the Soviets must also become more and more crippled. Without general elections, without unrestricted freedom of Press and Assembly, without a free struggle of opinion, life dies out in every public institution, becomes a mere semblance of life, in which only the bureaucracy remains as the active element. Public life gradually falls asleep, a few dozen party leaders of inexhaustible energy and boundless experience direct and rule. Among them, in reality, only a dozen outstanding heads do the leading and an elite of the working class is invited from time to time to meetings where they are to applaud the speeches of the leaders, and to approve proposed resolutions unanimously —at bottom, then, a clique affair—a dictatorship, to be sure, not the dictatorship of the proletariat, however, but only the dictatorship of a handful of politicians, that is a dictatorship in the bourgeois sense, in the sense of the rule of the Jacobins . . . ' (*Russ.,* pp. 47-48.)

Rosa Luxemburg's criticism of the Russian Revolution, as with all her writing, could give no solace to reformist critics of revolutionary socialism, but could serve as an aid to those who desire to keep the science of working-class action living and untrammelled. Her criticism of the Bolshevik party is in the best traditions of Marxism, of the basic maxim of Karl Marx: ' . . . merciless criticism of all things existing . . . '

'The Accumulation of Capital'

During the years 1906-1913, Rosa Luxemburg lectured on political economy at a German Social-Democratic Party school of activists. While doing so she prepared a book on Marxian economics entitled *Introduction to Political Economy*. When about to conclude the basic draft she met with an unexpected difficulty: 'I could not succeed in depicting the total process of capitalist production in all its practical relations and with its objective historical limitations with sufficient clarity. Closer examination of the matter then convinced me that it was a question of rather more than the mere art of representation, and that a problem remained to be solved which is connected with the theoretical matter of Volume II of Marx's *Capital* and at the same time closely connected with present-day imperialist politics and their economic roots.'

In this way Rosa Luxemburg came to write her major theoretical work, *The Accumulation of Capital. A Contribution to an Economic Explanation of Imperialism* (Berlin, 1913). The book is not at all easy to follow, especially for anyone not conversant with Marx's *Capital*. At the same time, without doubt, Rosa Luxemburg's contribution, whether one agrees with it or not, is one of the most, if not the most, important and original contributions to Marxian economic doctrine since *Capital*.

Marx, in analysing the laws of motion of capitalism, abstracted from it all non-capitalist factors, in the same way as a scientist studying the law of gravity would study it in a vacuum.

The problem with which Rosa Luxemburg deals is as follows: Can enlarged reproduction, ie, production on an increasing scale, take place under the conditions of abstract, pure capitalism, where non-capitalist countries do not exist, or where any classes besides capitalists and workers do not exist? Marx assumed that it can. Rosa Luxemburg argued that while in general, for the purposes of the analysis of capitalist economy, abstraction from non-capitalist factors is justified, it is **not** justified when dealing with the question of enlarged reproduction.

The question is, of course, purely theoretical, as in fact pure capitalism has never existed: enlarged reproduction has always taken place while capitalism has been invading pre-capitalist spheres, either inside the capitalist country itself—invasion into feudalism with the destruction of peasants, artisans, etc.—or into wholly agricultural, pre-capitalist countries.

If capitalism has never existed in pure form, one may well ask: What is the importance of the question whether enlarged reproduction is theoretically possible in pure capitalism? After all, neither Marx nor Rosa Luxemburg assumed that capitalism would continue to exist until **all** pre-capitalist formations had been overthrown. However, the answer to this question may throw light on the effect of the non-capitalist sphere on the accentuation or mitigation of the contradictions in capitalism, and on the factors impelling capitalism to imperialist expansion.

Let us begin by explaining how Marx described the process of reproduction as a whole under capitalism.

Marx starts with an analysis of simple reproduction, ie. on the assumption—which, of course, could never exist under capitalism—that there is no accumulation of capital, that the whole of the surplus value is spent on the personal consumption of the capitalists, production thus not expanding.

For the capitalist to carry on simple reproduction certain conditions must exist. He must be able to sell the product of his factory, and with the money obtained buy the means of production (machines, raw materials, etc,) that he needs for his particular industry; also he must get the labour power he needs from the market, as well as the means of consumption required to feed, clothe, and provide other necessities for the labourers. The product produced by the workers with the help of the means of production must again find a market, and so on.

While from the standpoint of the individual capitalist it makes no difference what his factory produces, whether machinery, stockings, or newspapers, provided he can find buyers for his product so that he can realise his capital plus the surplus value, to the capitalist economy as a whole it is extremely important that the total produce will be made up of certain determined use values, in other words, the total product must provide the means of production necessary to renew the process of production and the means of consumption needed by the workers and capitalists. The quantities of the different products can not be arbitrarily determined: the means of production produced must be equal in value to the size of the constant capital **c**: the means of consumption produced must be equal in value to the size of the wages bill—the variable capital **v**—plus the surplus value **s**.

To analyse simple reproduction Marx divided industry as a whole into two basic departments: that producing means of production (Department I) and that producing means of consumption (Department II). Between these two departments a certain proportionality must obtain for simple reproduction to take place. It is clear, for instance, that if Department I produced more machines than this department together with Department II needed, machinery would be over-produced, production in Department I consequently paralysed, and a whole sequence of events would follow from this. Similarly, if Department I produced too few machines, reproduction instead of repeating itself on the same level, would retrogress. The same would apply to Department II if it produced more or less means of consumption than the combined wages bill, or variable capital, and surplus value **(v + s)** in both departments.* The proportion between the demand for means of production and that for means of consumption in the economy as a whole depends on the ratio between the portion of capital devoted to the purchase of machinery and raw materials, ie, on the constant capital **(c)** of the whole economy on the one hand, and that portion of capital expended on paying wages, **v**, plus the profits of the capitalists in the whole economy.

In other words the products of Department I **(P1)** must be equal to the constant capital of Department I **(c1)** plus the constant capital of Department II **(c2)**:

$$P1 = c1 + c2.$$

Similarly the products of Department II **(P2)** must be equal to wages and surplus value in both departments together:

$$P2 = v1 + s1 + v2 + s2.$$

These two equations can be combined in one equation:

$$c2 = v1 + s1.$$

In other words, the value of machinery and raw materials, etc., needed

---

* Actually, what is needed for smooth reproduction is not only that a certain proportionality be kept between the production of Department I and that of Department II in the whole economy, but that the proportionality between the departments be kept also in every branch of the economy. Thus, for instance, the production of clothing machinery (Department I) will need to fit the demand for this kind of machinery in the clothing industry (Department II).

by Department II must be equal to the wages plus surplus value of workers and capitalists in Department I.

These equations are for simple reproduction. The formulae for enlarged reproduction are more complicated. Here part of the surplus value is expended on the personal consumption of the capitalists—this we shall denote by the letter **r**—and part is accumulated—this we shall denote by the letter **a. a** itself is divided into two portions: part serves to buy added means of production, ie, is spent on adding to available constant capital—**ac**—and part goes to pay wages to workers newly employed in production—**av**.

If the social demand for means of production under simple reproduction were expressed by the formula **c1 + c2**, enlarged reproduction would be expressed as **c1 + ac1 + c2 + ac2**.
Similarly the social demand for consumer goods, from
v1 + s1 + v2 + s2
becomes:
v1 + r1 + av1 + v2 + r2 + av2.
Hence the conditions necessary for enlarged reproduction can be formulated thus:
P1 = c1 + ac1 + c2 + ac2
P2 = v1 + r1 + av1 + v2 + r2 + av2
Or:
c2 + ac2 = v1 + r1 + av1.*
Now for Rosa Luxemburg's criticism of Marx's schemas.** Rosa

---

* These equations, which are algebraic formulations of Marx's analysis in Volume II of *Capital* were formulated by N. Bukharin in his *Der Imperialismus und die Akkumulation Das Kapitals* (Berlin, 1925) and we find them very useful for summing up Marx's many arithmetical examples.
** Before describing Rosa Luxemburg's analysis of reproduction, it must be clear that she **did not** develop a theory explaining the cyclical movement of boom, crisis and slump. She took it that the periodical cycles are phases of reproduction in capitalist economy, but not the whole of the process. Therefore, she abstracted her analysis from the cycles in order to study the process of reproduction in purity and as a whole. As she writes: ' . . . in spite of the sharp rises and falls in the course of a cycle, in spite of crises, the needs of society are always satisfied more or less, reproduction continues on its complicated course, and productive capacities develop progressively. How can this take place, leaving cycles and crises out of consideration? Here the real question begins . . . When we speak of capitalist reproduction in the following exposition, we shall always understand by this term a mean volume of productivity which is an average taken over the various phases of a cycle.' (*Acc.,* pp. 36-7.)

Luxemburg showed that a comparison of the formula for simple reproduction with that for enlarged reproduction produced a paradox. In the case of simple reproduction $c2$ must be equal to $v1 + s1$. In the case of enlarged reproduction, $c2 + ac2$ must be equal to $v1 + r1 + av1$. Now $v1 + r1 + av1$ are smaller than $v1 + s1$ (as $ac1$ is deducted from $s1$). So that if equilibrium were achieved under conditions of simple reproduction, the transition to enlarged reproduction would demand not only non-accumulation in Department II but the absurd position of disaccumulation.

And it is no accident, she said, that when Marx used diagrams to illustrate enlarged reproduction, he gave a smaller figure for $c2$ than the one he used to illustrate simple reproduction.

'Diagram of Simple Reproduction
'I   4000c + 1000v + 1000s = 6000
'II   2000c + 500v +   500s = 3000
                    Total   9000.

'Initial Diagram for Accumulation on an Expanded Scale
'I   4000c + 1000v + 1000s = 6000
'II   1500c + 750v +   750s = 3000
                    Total   9000.'
(*Capital*, Vol. II, p. 596.)

Thus the constant capital of Department II is 500 smaller in enlarged than in simple reproduction.

Marx goes on to elaborate the diagram of enlarged reproduction and he shows that, assuming that in Department I as well as in Department II no change in the organic composition of capital (ie, in the ratio of constant capital to variable capital) takes place, that the rate of exploitation remains constant, and that half the surplus value in Department I is capitalised, then the reproduction of capital will result in the following progression:

First year	I	4400c	+	1100v	+	1100s	=	6600
	II	1600c	+	800v	+	800s	=	3200
						Total		**9800**
Second year	I	4840c	+	1210v	+	1210s	=	7260
	II	1760c	+	880v	+	880s	=	3520
						Total		**10780**

Third year	I	5324c	+	1331v	+	1331s	=	7986
	II	1936c	+	968v	+	968s	=	3872
						Total		11858

Fourth year	I	5856c	+	1464v	+	1464s	=	8784
	II	2129c	+	1065v	+	1065s	=	4259
						Total		13043

Fifth year	I	6442c	+	1610v	+	1610s	=	9662
	II	2342c	+	1172v	+	1172s	=	4686
						Total		14348

(*Capital*, Vol. II, pp. 598-600.)

Analysing the above diagram, Rosa Luxemburg correctly points out a peculiarity they show: 'While in Department I half the surplus value is capitalised every time, and the other half consumed, so that there is an orderly expansion both of production and of personal consumption by the capitalists, the twofold process in Department II takes the following erratic course:

First year	150 are capitalised,	600 consumed
Second	240	660
Third	254	626
Fourth	290	678
Fifth	320	745

And she adds: 'Needless to say, the absolute figures of the diagram are arbitrary in every equation, but that does not detract from their scientific value. It is the **quantitative ratios** which are relevant, since they are supposed to express strictly determinate relationships. Those precise logical rules that lay down the relations of accumulation in Department I, seem to have been gained at the cost of any kind of principle in construing these relations for Department II; and this circumstance calls for a revision of the immanent connections revealed by the analysis.' (*Acc.*, p. 122.)

'Here there is no rule in evidence for accumulation and consumption to follow; both are wholly subservient to the requirements of accumulation in Department I.' (*Acc.*, p. 122.)

As regards the progress of the enlarged reproduction, if we assumed that in Department II as well as in Department I, there was an orderly expansion of both capital accumulation, and of the personal consumption of the capitalists, there would then have appeared an increasing disequilibrium between the two departments.

Rosa Luxemburg therefore shows clearly that if any logical rules were laid down for the relations of accumulation in Department I, these rules seem to 'have been gained at the cost of any kind of principle in constructing these relations for Department II'; or otherwise, if the same logical rules were applied to the relations of accumulation in Department II as those applied in Department I, a disequilibrium in the form of overproduction in Department II would appear and grow progressively.

It will now be easy to show, assuming as a point of departure for enlarged reproduction that the constant capital in Department II was not 500 smaller than in simple reproduction, that there would have been disequilibrium between Department I and Department II: the demand of Department I for means of consumption would have been 500 smaller at the beginning of the process than the supply available in Department II of the means of consumption looking for exchange: there would have been overproduction of consumer goods to the value of 500 at the start of the process of enlarged reproduction.

If Rosa Luxemburg did not abstract from a number of other factors, such as the rise in the rate of exploitation and the rise in the organic composition of capital, her argument would have been even stronger. It is easy to prove that if the rate of exploitation rises, so that the ratio of surplus value to wage ($s{:}v$) is rising, the relative demand for consumer goods as against producer goods will decline, and hence either the rate of accumulation in Department II would be even more erratic than in Marx's diagrams, or increasing surpluses would appear in Department II. Any rise in the portion of the surplus value accumulated would work in the same direction, as well as any growth of the organic composition of capital.

The above-mentioned three tendencies—the rise in the rate of exploitation, rise in the rate of accumulation, and rise in the organic composition of capital—Marx assumed to be absolute and immanent laws of capitalism.

If these were taken into account, Rosa Luxemburg's contention that under pure capitalism economic disequilibrium would be an absolute, unavoidable, permanent phenomenon, would be greatly strengthened.

However, there is one important factor which cancels out all the above factors and is immanently connected with them: the rise in the relative weight of Department I as compared with Department II. The rise in the organic composition of capital, the improvement of technique, has been historically and logically connected with the rise of

Department I compared with Department II. Thus it was calculated that the ratio of net output of capital goods to that of consumer goods was in Britain as follows:
1851, 100:470; 1871, 100:390; 1901, 100:170; 1924, 100:150.
The figures for the United States were:
1850, 100:240; 1890, 100:150; 1920, 100:80.
The figures for Japan:
1900, 100:480; 1913, 100:270; 1925, 100:240.
(W S and E S Woytinsky, *World Population and Production*, New York, 1953, pp. 415-416.)

To show that the rise in Department I compared with Department II counteracts the factors mentioned by Rosa Luxemburg (as well as those added by the present writer to strengthen Rosa Luxemburg's argument about the tendency of overproduction in Department II), some diagrammatic representation of the effect of the change in the relative weight of Department I to Department II on the exchange relationship between the two departments will be given.

The capital invested in Department I can grow comparatively to Department II in two ways:
1. by having a higher rate of accumulation in Department I than in Department II;
2. by the transference of capital from Department II to Department I.
We shall give a diagrammatic example for each of these two processes.

Let us assume that the rate of accumulation in Department I is higher than in Department II, say, half the surplus value in Department I compared with only a third in Department II. We shall assume also that the other factors (the rate of exploitation at 100 per cent, the organic composition of capital where constant capital is five times bigger than variable capital) remain unchanged. Then, using Marx's diagram quoted above as a point of departure, the reproduction of capital will result in the following progression (figures are rounded for simplicity):

Point of departure:
I $5000c + 1000v + 1000s = 7000$
II $1500c + 300v + 300s = 2100$
End of first year:
I $5000c + 1000v + 500r + 417ac + 83av = 7000$
II $1500c + 300v + 200r + 80ac + 20av = 2100$
$c2 + ac2 = 1580$
while $v1 + r1 + av1 = 1583$.

Thus at the end of the first year, instead of a surplus in Department II as presumed by Rosa Luxemburg, a surplus appears in Department I, amounting to 3.

End of second year:

I $\quad$ 5417c + 1083v + 541r + 450ac + 90av = 7583

II $\quad$ 1580c + 320v + 213r + 90ac + 18av = 2220

c2 + ac2 = 1670

while v1 + r1 + av1 = 1714

the surplus in Department I is now 44.

End of third year:

I $\quad$ 5867c + 1173v + 586r + 489ac + 98av = 8213

II $\quad$ 1670c + 338v + 225r + 94ac + 19av = 2346

c2 + ac2 = 1764

while v1 + r1 + av1 = 1857

the surplus in Department I is now 93.

From the above diagrams it is clear that if we assume that the rate of exploitation and the organic composition of capital remain unchanged, while the rate of accumulation in Department I is higher than in Department II then overproduction appears in Department I.*

As we have said above, Department I can increase relatively to Department II also by transference of surplus value from Department II to Department I. Let us illustrate this process diagrammatically. We shall assume that the rate of exploitation, the organic composition of capital and the rate of accumulation are the same in both departments and they remain unchanged. At the same time, we shall assume that half the surplus value produced in Department II is being transferred to Department I.

The progress of enlarged production could then be described by the following diagrams:

Point of departure:

I $\quad$ 5000c + 1000v + 1000s = 7000

II $\quad$ 1500c + 300v + 300s = 2100

End of first year:

I $\quad$ 5000c + 1000v + 500r + 417ac + 83av = 7000

II $\quad$ 1500c + 300v + 150r + 63ac + 12av (plus surplus value

* Rosa Luxemburg's argument against exactly this idea of a higher rate of accumulation in Department I than in Department II (*Acc.*, pp. 338-9) is absolutely wrong. We have not the space to deal with it here. The reader should consult the source.

transferred to Department I: **63ac + 12av) = 2100**
c2 + ac2 = 1563
while **v1 + r1 + av1** (plus the **av** transferred from Department II) = **1595**.
Thus at the end of the first year, instead of a surplus in Department II
as presumed by Rosa Luxemburg, we are faced with overproduction in
Department I amounting to 32.

End of second year:
I   **5480c + 1095v + 547r + 455ac + 91av = 7670**
II   **1563c + 312v + 156r + 65ac + 13av** (plus surplus value
transferred to Department I: **65ac + 13av**) = **2187**
c2 + ac2 = 1628
while **v1 + r1 + av1** (plus the **av** transferred from Department II) = **1746**.
The surplus in Department I is 118.

End of third year:
I   **6000c + 1200v + 600r + 500ac + 100av = 8400**
II   **1628c + 325v + 162r + 67ac + 14av** (plus surplus value
transferred to Department I: **67ac + 14av**) = **2278**
c2 + ac2 = 1695
while **v1 + r1 + av1** (plus the **av** transferred from Department II) = **1914**.
The surplus in Department I is 219.

Now Rosa Luxemburg argues against this idea that the transfer of
surplus value from one department to another can help to bring about
an exchange balance between the departments, saying that the 'intended
transfer of part of the capitalised surplus value from Department II to
Department I is ruled out, first because the material form of this surplus
value is obviously useless to Department I, and secondly because of the
relations of exchange between the two departments which would in
turn necessitate an equivalent transfer of the products of Department I
into Department II.' (*Acc.*, pp. 340-341.) In other words, Rosa
Luxemburg argues that Marx's schema is based on the assumption that
the realisation of surplus value can take place only through an exchange
between departments, and secondly that the presumed surplus in
Department II takes a natural form, ie, remains as means of consumption,
and **cannot** serve directly as means of production. Now the first
argument falls through owing to the fact that exchange between enterprises in the same department can serve to realise the surplus value: when
an owner of a hat factory sells his hats to workers who produce biscuits,
he realises the surplus value produced by his workers. Secondly, quite a
large number of consumer goods can serve also as means of production:

if a building contractor builds factories instead of flats, this signifies the transference of capital from Department II to Department I; electricity can serve to light flats as well as to move machinery; grain can feed man (consumption) as well as pigs (productive consumption), etc. Thirdly, without the possibility of transference of capital from one department to another, the postulate that the rate of profit throughout the economy tends to equality, which is basic Marxian economics, loses its foundation.

From the diagrams given above it becomes clear that a relative increase of Department I compared with Department II, if all other conditions remain unchanged, brings in its wake surpluses in the exchange relations in Department I.

Can this factor not counteract the one pointed out by Rosa Luxemburg to be the cause of a surplus in Department II? Are the different counteracting factors not in fact two sides of one coin, the progress of capitalist economy? Of course this is so.

Rosa Luxemburg came to the conclusion that a surplus must appear in Department II because she paid attention to only one side of the coin. Considering both sides, it is clear that it is possible in pure capitalism for proportionality between the two departments to exist, while the accumulation in both is regular, not erratic.

However, the theoretical **possibility** of the preservation of correct proportionalities between the two departments, which will prevent over-production by their mutual exchange while accumulation goes forward on an even keel, does not mean that in actual life the anarchic and atomistic working of capitalism leads to continuous and stable preservation of the proportionalities needed. And here the factor Rosa Luxemburg pointed to—the existence of non-capitalist formations into which capitalism expands—is extremely important. If it is not a pre-requisite for enlarged reproduction as Rosa Luxemburg argued, it is, at least, a factor that eases the process of enlarged reproduction, of accumulation, by making the interdependence of the two departments less than absolute. One cannot but agree with Rosa Luxemburg when she says: 'Accumulation is more than an internal relationship between the branches of capitalist economy'; as a result of the relationship between the capitalist and non-capitalist environment 'the two great departments of production sometimes perform the accumulative process on their own, independently of each other, but even then at every step the movements overlap and intersect. From this we get most complicated relations, divergencies in the speed and direction of accumulation for the two departments, different relations with non-capitalist modes of production as regards both material elements and elements of value . . . ' (*Acc.*, p. 417.)

As a matter of fact, the number of factors determining whether certain proportionalities between the departments lead to equilibrium or not are numerous and contradictory (the rate of exploitation, the rate of accumulation in different industries, changes in the organic composition of capital in different industries, and so on.) and, once the economy leaves the state of equilibrium, what was proportionality before, turns into disproportionality with snowball effect. Hence the exchange between capitalist industry and the non-capitalist sphere, even if it is small in absolute terms, may have a tremendous effect on the elasticity and hence stability, of capitalism.

In her book Rosa Luxemburg goes backwards and forwards between analyses of the schemas of reproduction—which describe exchange relationships between the two departments of industry—and another set of relations between the two departments: the **potentiality** of means of production to become means of consumption—means of production not only being **exchanged** for means of consumption, but in time being realised in new means of consumption. The proportionalities expressed in Marx's schemas are conditions without which accumulation **cannot** take place; but in order that accumulation **should actually take place** there is need for a progressively enlarged demand for commodities, and the question that arises is: where does this demand come from?

Capitalist prosperity depends upon the increasing output and absorption of capital goods. But this depends in the last analysis upon the capacity of industry to sell an increasing output of consumer goods. However, in trying to sell its products, capitalist industry enters into deepening contradictions, the most fundamental of which is that between production and the limited market: 'The last cause of all real crises always remains the poverty and restricted consumption of the masses as compared to the tendency of capitalist production to develop the productive forces in such a way, that only the absolute power of consumption of the entire society would be their limit.' (*Capital*, Vol. III, p. 568.)

Rosa Luxemburg argued that the factor making it possible for capitalism to get away from the absolute impediment to accumulation of the limiting market was the penetration of capitalist industry into the non-capitalist territories.*

---

* A different 'Marxist' answer to the capitalist dilemma was given by Otto Bauer in his criticism of Rosa Luxemburg's book. Using much more complicated schemes of reproduction than Marx or Rosa Luxemburg, he tried to prove that 'the accumulation of capital adapts itself to the increase of population': 'the periodic

Rosa Luxemburg, more than any Marxist or non-Marxist economist, drew attention to the effect of the non-capitalist frontier on capitalism. Relying on this factor—even if she herself did not develop all the main consequences of it—one can try and sum up the effect of the expansion of capitalism into non-capitalist territories thus:

1. The markets of the backward colonial countries, by increasing demand for goods from the industrial countries, weaken the tendency for overproduction there, decrease the reserve army of unemployed, and so bring about an improvement in the wages of workers in the industrial countries.

2. The increase in wages brought about in this way has a cumulative effect. By increasing the internal market in the industrial countries, the tendency for overproduction is weakened, unemployment decreases, wages rise.

3. The export of capital adds to the prosperity of the industrial countries as it creates a market for their goods—at least temporarily. The export of cotton goods from Britain to India presupposes that India is able to pay for it straight away, by exporting cotton, for instance. On the other hand, the export of capital for the building of a railway presupposes an export of goods—rails, locomotives, etc.—beyond the immediate purchasing power, or exporting power of India. In other words, **for a time**, the export of capital is an important factor in enlarging markets for the industries of the advanced countries. However, in time, this factor turns into its opposite: capital once exported puts a brake on the export of goods from the 'mother' country after the colonial countries start to pay profit or interest on it. In order to pay a profit of £10 million to Britain (on British capital invested in India) India has to import less than it exports, and thus save the money needed to the tune of £10 million. In other words, the act of exporting capital from Britain to India expands the market for British goods; the payment of interest and profit on existing British capital in India restricts the markets for British goods.

Hence the existence of great British capital investments abroad does not at all exclude overproduction and mass unemployment in Britain.

---

cycle of prosperity, crisis and slump in an empirical expression of the fact that the capitalist apparatus of production automatically overcomes too large or too small accumulation by adapting anew the accumulation of capital to the increase of population.' (*NZ*, 1913, p. 871.) And this is said not by a disciple of Malthus, but of Marx, for whom the primary factor should not be population increase but capital accumulation!

Contrary to Lenin's view, the high profit from capital invested abroad may well be not a concomitant of capitalist prosperity and stabilisation in the imperialist country, but a factor of mass unemployment and depression.

4. The export of capital to the colonies affects the whole capital market in the imperialist country. Even if the surplus of capital looking vainly for investment were very small, its cumulative influence could be tremendous, as it would create pressure in the capital markets, and strengthen the downward trend of the rate of profit. This in turn would have a cumulative effect of its own on the activity of capital, on the entire economic activity, on employment, and so on the purchasing power of the masses, and so again in a vicious circle, on the markets.

The export of surplus capital can obviate these difficulties and can thus be of great importance to the whole of capitalist prosperity, and thus to reformism.

5. By thus relieving pressure in capital markets the export of capital diminishes competition between different enterprises, and so diminishes the need of each to rationalise and modernise its equipment. (This to some extent explains the technical backwardness of British industry, the pioneer of the industrial revolution, as compared with that of Germany today, for example). This weakens the tendencies to overproduction and unemployment, wage cuts, and so on. (Of course, in changed circumstances, in which Britain has ceased to hold a virtual monopoly in the industrial world, this factor may well cause the defeat of British industry in the world market, unemployment and cuts in wages.)

6. Buying cheap raw materials and foodstuffs in the colonies allows real wages in the industrial countries to be increased without cutting into the rate of profit. This increase of wages means widened domestic markets **without** a decrease in the rate and amount of profit, in other words, without weakening the motive of capitalist production.

7. The period during which the agrarian colonial countries serve to broaden markets for the industrial countries will no longer be in proportion to

   a. the size of the colonial world compared with the productive power of the advanced industrial countries, and

   b. the extent that the industrialisation of the former is postponed.

8. All the beneficial effects of imperialism on capitalist prosperity would disappear if there were no national boundaries between the industrial imperialist countries and their colonies. Britain

exported goods and capital to India and imported cheap raw materials and foodstuffs, but it did not let the unemployed of India—increased by the invasion of British capitalism—enter Britain's labour market. If not for the barrier (a financial one) to mass Indian immigration into Britain, wages in Britain would not have risen throughout the last century. The crisis of capitalism would have got deeper and deeper. Reformism would not have been able to replace revolutionary Chartism.*

One may agree or disagree with Rosa Luxemburg's criticism of Marx's schemas in Volume II of *Capital,* and with all or some of the links in her chain of reasoning leading to the final conclusion that if the capitalist mode of production was not only the predominant one but the only one, of necessity in a short time capitalism would have collapsed from its internal contradictions. Whatever one thinks, one cannot doubt the tremendous service Rosa Luxemburg did in drawing attention to the effect of non-capitalist spheres on the stability of capitalism. As Professor Joan Robinson states in her introductory essay to the English edition of the *Accumulation of Capital:* ' . . . few would deny that the extension of capitalism into new territories was the main-spring of what an academic economist has called the 'vast secular boom' of the last two hundred years, and many academic economists account for the uneasy condition of capitalism in the twentieth century largely by the 'closing of the frontier' all over the world.' (*Acc.,* p. 28.) Joan Robinson mixes praise of Rosa Luxemburg's analysis with a criticism that Rosa Luxemburg ignored the rise in real wages that occurred throughout the capitalist world—a factor enlarging the market—and thus presented an incomplete picture. However, even if Rosa Luxemburg did not include this factor in her analysis—and it is extraneous to the main line of her argument about the possibility or impossibility of enlarged reproduction in pure capitalism—one cannot explain the rise in real wages itself independently of the main feature Rosa Luxemburg pointed out: the expansion of capitalism into non-capitalist spheres.**

* By the way, the 'third' buyer—not worker nor capitalist consumer—need not necessarily be the non-capitalist producer, but the non-producing state; hence the permanent war economy can, at least for a time, have a similar effect on capitalist prosperity as the non-capitalist economic sphere. (See T Cliff, 'Perspectives of the Permanent War Economy', *Socialist Review,* May, 1957.)

** In her argument Rosa Luxemburg made a number of side errors which were discovered subsequently by N Bukharin in his *Der Imperialismus und die Akkumulation des Kapitals,* although he did not disprove her central thesis (even though he thought he did). Thus, for instance, Rosa Luxemburg devoted a good deal of attention to purely monetary problems of capital accumulation—whether, for instance, one should include the production of money commodity (gold, silver, etc.) in Department I, as Marx did, or, as she herself proposed, should add a third department. It seems that in a number of places in her book, Rosa Luxemburg confuses the question: Where does the **demand** come from? with the question: Where does the **money** come from? But as this is of only secondary importance to her main thesis, we shall not deal with it here. Again, while, if we carefully followed Rosa Luxemburg's own reasoning about the schemes of reproduction, we should say that the weight of her argument is that **a portion of** the surplus value in Department II could not be realised under pure capitalism, Rosa Luxemburg herself sums up the argument as if she proved that no realisation of any portion of the surplus value could take place under pure capitalism. (This was pointed out by F Sternberg, in *Der Imperialismus*, Berlin, 1926, p. 102.)

Rosa Luxemburg's place in history

Franz Mehring, the biographer of Marx, did not exaggerate when he called Rosa Luxemburg the best brain after Marx. But she did not contribute her brain alone to the working-class movement; she gave everything she had—her heart, her passion, her strong will, her very life.

Above all else, Rosa Luxemburg was a revolutionary socialist. And among the great revolutionary socialist leaders and teachers she has a special historical place of her own.

When reformism degraded the socialist movements by aspiring purely for the 'welfare state', by tinkering with capitalism, it became of first importance to make a revolutionary criticism of this handmaiden of capitalism. It is true that other Marxist teachers besides Rosa Luxemburg—Lenin, Trotsky, Bukharin and others—conducted a revolutionary fight against reformism. But they had a limited front to fight against. In their country, Russia, the roots of this weed were so weak and thin, that a mere tug was sufficient to uproot it. Where Siberia or the gallows stared every socialist or democrat in the face, who in principle could oppose the use of violence by the labour movement? Who in Tsarist Russia would have dreamed of a parliamentary road to socialism? Who could advocate a policy of coalition government, for with whom could coalitions be made? Where trade unions scarcely existed, who could think of considering them the panacea of the labour movement? Lenin, Trotsky and the other Russian Bolshevik leaders did not need to counter the arguments of reformism with a painstaking and exact analysis. All they needed was a broom to sweep it away to the dungheap of history.

In Central and Western Europe conservative reformism had much deeper roots, a much more embracing influence on the thoughts and moods of the workers. The arguments of the reformists had to be answered by superior ones, and here Rosa Luxemburg excelled. In these countries her scalpel is a much more useful weapon than Lenin's sledgehammer.

In Tsarist Russia the mass of the workers were not organised in parties or trade unions. There there was not such a threat of powerful empires being built by a bureaucracy rising from the working class as in the well-organised workers' movement of Germany; and it was natural that Rosa Luxemburg had a much earlier and clearer view of the role of the labour bureaucracy than Lenin or Trotsky. She understood long before they did that the only power that could break through bureaucratic chains is the initiative of the workers. Her writings on this subject can serve as an inspiration to workers in the advanced industrial countries, and are a more valuable contribution to the struggle to liberate the workers from the pernicious ideology of bourgeois reformism than those of any other Marxist.

In Russia, where the Bolsheviks were always a large and important part of the organised socialists, even if they were not always the majority, as their name signifies, the question of the attitude of a small Marxist minority to a mass, conservatively led organisation, never really rose as a problem. It remained for Rosa Luxemburg largely to develop the right approach to this vital question. Her guiding principle was: stay with the masses throughout their travail and try to help them. She therefore opposed abstention from the main stream of the labour movement, no matter what the level of its development. Her fight against sectarianism is extremely important for the labour movement of the West, especially at present, when welfare-stateism is such an all-pervading sentiment. The British Labour movement, in particular, having suffered from the sectarianism of Hyndman and the SDF, later the BSP and SLP, then the Communist Party (especially in its 'third period') and now further sects, can gain inspiration from Rosa Luxemburg for a principled fight against reformism, which does not degenerate into flight from it. She taught that a revolutionary should not swim with the stream of reformism, nor sit outside it and look in the opposite direction, but swim against it.

Rosa Luxemburg's conception of the structure of the revolutionary organisations—that they should be built, from below up, on a consistently democratic basis—fits the needs of the workers' movement in the advanced countries much more closely than Lenin's conception of 1902-4 which was copied and given an added bureaucratic twist by the Stalinists the world over.

She understood more clearly than anyone that the structure of the revolutionary party, and the mutual relation between the party and the class, would have a big influence, not only on the struggle against capitalism and for workers' power, but also on the fate of this power itself. She stated prophetically that without the widest workers' democracy 'officials behind their desks' would replace the workers' hold on political power. 'Socialism,' she said, 'cannot be decreed or introduced by edict.'

Rosa Luxemburg's blend of revolutionary spirit and clear understanding of the nature of the labour movement in Western and Central Europe is in some way connected with her particular background of birth in the Tsarist Empire, long residence in Germany, and full activity in both the Polish and German labour movements. Anyone of smaller stature would have been assimilated into one of the two environments, but not Rosa Luxemburg. To Germany she brought the 'Russian' spirit, the spirit of revolutionary action. To Poland and Russia she brought the 'Western' spirit of workers' self-reliance, democracy and self-emancipation.

Her *Accumulation of Capital* is an invaluable contribution to Marxism. In dealing with the mutual relations between the industrially advanced countries and the backward agrarian ones she brought out the most important idea that imperialism, while stabilising capitalism over a long period, at the same time threatens to bury humanity under its ruins.

Being vital, energetic and non-fatalistic in her approach to history, which she conceived of as the fruit of human activity, and at the same time laying bare the deep contradictions of capitalism, Rosa Luxemburg did not consider that the victory of socialism was inevitable. Capitalism, she thought, could be either the ante-chamber to socialism or the brink of barbarism. We who live in the shadow of the H-bomb must comprehend this warning and use it as a spur to action.

In the late nineteenth and early twentieth centuries the German labour movement, with decades of peace behind it, sank under the illusion that this situation was everlasting. We who are in the throes of discussion about controlled disarmament, United Nations, Summit Meetings, could do no better than learn from Rosa Luxemburg's clear analysis of the unbreakable tie between war and capitalism, and her insistence that the fight for peace is inseparable from the fight for socialism.

A passion for truth made Rosa Luxemburg recoil from any dogmatic thought. In a period when Stalinism has largely turned Marxism into a dogma, spreading desolation in the field of ideas, Rosa

Luxemburg's writings are invigorating and life-giving. Nothing was more intolerable to her than bowing down to 'infallible authorities'. As a real disciple of Marx she was able to think and act independently of her master. Though grasping the spirit of his teaching, she did not lose her critical faculties in a simple repetition of his words, whether these fitted the changed situation or not, whether they were right or wrong. Rosa Luxemburg's independence of thought is the greatest inspiration to socialists everywhere and always. In consequence, no one would have denounced more forcefully than she herself any effort to canonise her, to turn her into an 'infallible authority', a leader of a school of thought or action. She loved the conflict of ideas as a means of coming nearer to the truth.

During a period when so many who consider themselves Marxists sap Marxism of its deep humanistic content, no one can do more to release us from the chains of lifeless mechanistic materialism than Rosa Luxemburg. For Marx communism (or socialism) was 'real humanism', 'a society in which the full and free development of every individual is the ruling principle.' (*Capital,* Vol. I. p. 649.) Rosa Luxemburg was the embodiment of these humanistic passions. Sympathy with the lowly and oppressed were central motives of her life. Her deep emotion and feeling for the suffering of people and all living things expressed themselves in everything she did or wrote, whether in her letters from prison or in the deepest writings of her theoretical research.

Rosa Luxemburg, however, well knew that where human tragedy is on an epic scale, tears won't help. Her motto, like that of Spinoza, might have been: 'Do not cry, do not laugh, but understand', even though she herself had her full share of tears and laughter. Her method was to reveal the trends of development in social life in order to help the working class to use its potentialities in the best possible way in conjunction with objective development. She appealed to man's reason rather than to emotion.

Deep human sympathy and an earnest desire for truth, unbounded courage and a magnificent brain united in Rosa Luxemburg to make her a great revolutionary socialist. As her closest friend, Klara Zetkin, wrote in her obituary: 'In Rosa Luxemburg the socialist idea was a dominating and powerful passion of both heart and brain, a truly creative passion which burned ceaselessly. The great task and the overpowering ambition of this astonishing woman was to prepare the way for social revolution, to clear the path of history for Socialism. To experience the revolution, to fight its battles—that was the highest happiness for her. With a will, determination, selflessness and devotion for which words are too weak, she consecrated her whole life and her whole being to Socialism. She gave herself completely to the cause of Socialism, not only in her tragic death, but throughout her whole life, daily and hourly, through the struggles of many years . . . She was the sharp sword, the living flame of revolution.'

Suggested reading

There are two general collections of Rosa Luxemburg's writings in print. Both include **The Mass Strike, Reform or Revolution**, and **The Junius Pamphlet** besides much else: **Rosa Luxemburg Speaks**, edited by Mary Alice Waters (Pathfinder Press) and **Selected Political Writings**, edited by Dick Howard (Monthly Review Press). There is also **The National Question: Selected Writings by Rosa Luxemburg**, edited by Horace B Davis (Monthly Review Press). The following important individual works are currently in print in English: **The Mass Strike** (Merlin Press), **Reform or Revolution** (Pathfinder Press), **The Accumulation of Capital** (Routledge), **The Junius Pamphlet** (Merlin Press), and **What is Economics?** (Merlin Press).

There are two good biographies of Rosa Luxemburg: **Rosa Luxemburg: Ideas in Action**, by Paul Frölich (Pluto Press) and **Rosa Luxemburg**, by John Nettl (Oxford University Press). **The Legacy of Rosa Luxemburg**, by Norman Geras (New Left Books) contains useful essays on some aspects of her politics, particularly on her attitude to the nature of the Russian Revolution.

THE MASS STRIKE
by Rosa Luxemburg
The mass strike fuses together the struggle for reforms within the
capitalist system with the struggle for its revolutionary overthrow.
This classic book examines the mass strikes which came to their
climax with the Russian Revolution of 1905.
£1.95

THE LOST REVOLUTION: GERMANY 1918-23
by Chris Harman
Revolutions that are defeated are soon forgotten. Yet the defeat of
the huge working-class upheavals that shook Germany after the First
World War was a key link in the rise to power of both Hitler and
Stalin.
£5.95

MARXISM AND THE PARTY
by John Molyneux
The question of party organisation has been central for socialists for
more than a century. This book examines the work of Marx, Lenin,
Luxemburg, Trotsky and Gramsci on the party and its relationship to
the working class.
£4.50

THE WESTERN SOVIETS
Workers' Councils versus Parliament 1915-21
by Donny Gluckstein
When parliamentary channels of democracy failed the working class
early this century, allowing the slaughter of the First World War, the
workers' council movements of Germany, Britain, Italy and Russia
proposed an alternative mass democracy. This book enlightens a
little-known, but important period in our history.
£5.95

MARXISM AND TRADE UNION STRUGGLE
The General Strike of 1926
by Tony Cliff and Donny Gluckstein
The British 1926 General Strike put the political ideas of the day to
the ultimate test of practice. In the light cast by the solidarity of
millions of workers the treachery of the trade union leaders and the
weaknesses of Communist Party strategy were clearly outlined. This
book uses an examination of the strike to re-examine key questions
for socialists today.
£6.25

FESTIVAL OF THE OPPRESSED
Solidarity, reform and revolution in Poland 1980-81
by Colin Barker
The trade union Solidarity was the most impressive working-class movement the world had seen for half a century. This book not only recaptures its magnificent achievements, but brings new insights into the class forces that gave it birth and led to its suppression.
£4.25

CLASS STRUGGLE AND WOMEN'S LIBERATION
1640 to the present day
by Tony Cliff
Tony Cliff looks at the long struggle for women's liberation in a historical analysis that ranges from the Germany of Rosa Luxemburg and Clara Zetkin to the women's movements of Britain and the United States in the 1970s.
£4.50

WHAT IS THE REAL MARXIST TRADITION?
by John Molyneux
The hundred years since Marx's death have seen the emergence of innumerable 'Marxisms'. Social democracy, Stalinism and the Third World liberation movements, among others, claim the title. But what is the real Marxist tradition? This book untangles the knot.
£1.95

All available from good bookshops,
or by post from the publishers (add 15 per cent for postage).
BOOKMARKS
265 Seven Sisters Road, Finsbury Park, London N4 2DE, England.
PO Box 16085, Chicago, Illinois 60616, USA.
GPO Box 1473N, Melbourne 3001, Australia.

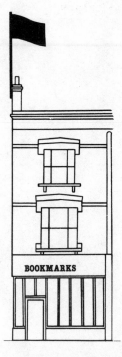

Bookmarks is a socialist bookshop in North London, where you'll find two floors of books on socialism, internationalism, trade unions, working-class history, economics, women's issues, socialist novels and much more. We're just around the corner from Finsbury Park tube station. If you live too far away to call in, we run a large socialist mail order service too, sending books all over the world. Just drop us a line for our latest booklists.

BOOKMARKS, 265 Seven Sisters Road, London N4 2DE, England.

FLAUBERT'S PARROT

Julian Barnes is the author of ten novels, including
Metroland, *A History of the World in 10½
Chapters*, *Staring at the Sun* and *Arthur &
George*; two books of short stories, *Cross Channel*
and *The Lemon Table*; and three collections of
journalism, *Letters from London*, *Something to
Declare* and *The Pedant in the Kitchen*. His most
recent book, *Nothing to be Frightened of*, was
published in 2008. His work has been translated
into more than thirty languages. In France he is the
only writer to have won both the Prix Médicis (for
Flaubert's Parrot) and the Prix Femina (for
Talking it Over). In 1993 he was awarded the
Shakespeare Prize by the FVS Foundation of
Hamburg. He lives in London.

ALSO BY JULIAN BARNES

Fiction

Metroland
Before She Met Me
Staring at the Sun
A History of the World in 10½ Chapters
Talking it Over
The Porcupine
Cross Channel
England, England
Love, etc
The Lemon Table
Arthur & George

Non-fiction

Letters from London 1990–1995
Something to Declare
The Pedant in the Kitchen
Nothing to be Frightened of

Translation

In the Land of Pain
by Alphonse Daudet

JULIAN BARNES

Flaubert's Parrot

VINTAGE BOOKS
London

Published by Vintage 2009

2 4 6 8 10 9 7 5 3 1

'Flaubert's Parrot' was first published in the *London Review of
Books*, and 'Emma Bovary's Eyes' first appeared, in an edited form,
in *Granta*

First published in Great Britain in 1984 by Jonathan Cape

Vintage
Random House, 20 Vauxhall Bridge Road,
London, SW1V 2SA

www.vintage-books.co.uk

Addresses for companies within The Random House Group Limited
can be found at: www.randomhouse.co.uk/offices.htm

The Random House Group Limited Reg. No. 954009

A CIP catalogue record for this book
is available from the British Library

ISBN 9780099540083

The Random House Group Limited supports The Forest
Stewardship Council (FSC), the leading international forest
certification organisation. All our titles that are printed on
Greenpeace approved FSC certified paper carry the FSC logo.
Our paper procurement policy can be found at:
www.rbooks.co.uk/environment

Printed and bound in Great Britain by
CPI Cox & Wyman, Reading , RG1 8EX